THE
PUFFIN

THE
PUFFIN

DAVID BOAG
AND
MIKE ALEXANDER

BLANDFORD

This paperback edition first published in by Blandford.
An imprint of the Cassell Group,
Wellington House, 125 Strand, London, WC2R OBB.

Previously published in the UK in hardback 1986 by
Blandford Press as *The Atlantic Puffin*.

Distribution in the United States
by Sterling Publishing Co., Inc.
387 Park Avenue South, New York,
NY 10016-8810

Distribution in Australia
by Capricorn Link (Australia) Pty Ltd
2/13 Carrington Road, Castle Hill NSW 2154

British Library Cataloguing in Publication Data

Boag, David
  The Atlantic Puffin
  1.Puffins
  I.Title II.Alexander, Mike
  598'.33   QL696.C42

ISBN 0-7137-2596-6

Printed and bound in Hong Kong by Dah Hua Printing Press Co.

To Janet and Rosanne

Contents

	Acknowledgements	8
	Introduction	9
1	Description and Distribution	18
2	Life at Sea	30
3	The Puffin Colony	44
4	Courtship and Egg-Laying	66
5	Chick Development	82
6	Mortality and Kleptoparasitism	100
7	Men and Puffins	111
	Appendices	
	1: Photographic Techniques	119
	2: Distribution of the Atlantic Puffin	124
	Further Reading	126
	Index	127

Acknowledgements

WHEN the idea of a book on the life of the puffin first came to me, I contacted Mike Alexander. Mike is a full-time warden of Skomer Island National Nature Reserve in Wales. He explained that he had had a similar idea and, after sharing our thoughts, we decided to work together. Much of the basic research was done by Mike, who lives on the island, whilst I did all of the writing. The photography we worked on together. Although the book is written in a personal way, the observations made in the text could be attributed to either Mike or myself.

However, a project of this type is never the work of just two people and there are many we would like to thank. The West Wales Trust for Nature Conservation and the Nature Conservancy Council kindly gave us permission to undertake the project, based on Skomer Island, and we are extremely grateful. We would also like to thank Nikon UK Ltd for the loan of a large and expensive lens.

The puffin has been extremely well researched by a large number of enthusiasts many of whom we have met through the years; perhaps they will accept our gratitude for the work they have done and the thoughts they have shared so freely. We would also like to acknowledge the tremendous amount of work carried out by Dr Mike Harris over many years and the excellent and useful papers he has written on puffins. Ruth Ashcroft spent several seasons on the island and we especially thank her for such reliable information, as well as many useful discussions.

Our enthusiasm for the puffin was shared by our wives and my son Paul. We are so grateful that they shared the difficult times with us, as well as the good. Janet shared my frustrations when writing the manuscript and then corrected and typed it. Rosanne spent many hours observing, recording and finally processing miles of film. For us to simply say thank you seems inadequate.

David Boag
Mike Alexander

Introduction

THE sun had not shared its warmth with the island for weeks but this morning it rose over the eastern side of the bay into a crystal-clear sky. The sea, which had not settled for months on end, now rested in a quiet calm. A gull drifted silently across the cliff face, following its own distorted shadow cast by the early morning sun. The only sounds to break the stillness were the piping calls of oystercatchers on the rocks beneath the cliff and the gentle lapping of the wavelets as they gurgled between the boulders. The stillness of the day was demonstrated by a whiff of smoke, rising vertically from the chimney of a lonely cottage which nestled into the cliff top. Far out at sea, a white speck appeared for a moment or two.

Within an hour, the silent gull had been joined by others of its kind on the west side of the bay yet, although they now squabbled amongst themselves over some trivial matter, their cries did not destroy the harmony of the island. The speck on the sea, which was in fact a puffin, was now only about a kilometre from the bay. As the puffin rolled on his side to scratch his head, his white belly caught the morning sunshine as it had an hour ago. He continued to preen for the next 20 minutes or so, not with any urgency but with a laziness of content that fitted the day.

It was not that he needed to arrange his feathers for quite so long but the air between them, and the warmth of the sun, felt good. He was not a lonely bird and so, having settled his plumage into place with a few violent wing flaps, he gently paddled his way to a group of puffins that had landed on the water about 15 metres in front of him. Feeling content to be with company, he tucked his head back under his wing to rest. Yet, even as he rested, every movement of his feet beneath the water took him a little closer to the island.

The 7 months since he had last seen the island had been a period of struggling against, or perhaps bending with, the forces of nature, for he was well adapted to do so. He had wintered 300 kilometres, sometimes 800 kilometres, to the west, far out in the North Atlantic. He knew the greyness of the sea in a howling gale, when the wind drove waves higher than the cottage on the cliff, slicing the tops off in a white spume, spraying his very soul with its chill.

Skomer Island, Wales, viewed from 1,500 metres. A typical puffin island.

Driving rain, sleet and hail were his constant companions, forcing his eyes to close against their battering power. Thunder, lightning, rain or hail, what did he care! A flick of his head and it was gone. It ran in rivulets off his back. Deep beneath the water was peace from the turmoil and a jolly good meal. He had already seen ten winters through; nothing had been different about this one. Even at this time of year, he enjoyed the company of other puffins during periods of comparative calm and, although for days on end waves would prevent them from seeing each other, they were never more than a kilometre or so apart. On occasions, groups of five or ten would gather together until the next storm split them up again. He enjoyed the wild sea as he enjoyed the island, each within its own season.

The puffin did not think of the days that had passed; he took each moment as it arrived and made the most of it. A puffin's nature is not to dwell on history.

He had drifted close to a young female and, removing his beak from beneath his wing, he flicked his head twice in a provocative manner. The female ignored his advances and so, swimming closer, he repeated the toss of his head. Confused at this strange behaviour, she began to paddle quickly away, preening at her wing feathers in an exaggerated fashion, as if to clear her thoughts of this strange male. He drifted away from the female for he did not really want her; he was only flirting to pass the time. He knew that, before long, his female would join him in the bay and then real courtship would begin.

By mid-day, the raft of puffins on the sea had increased in numbers; there were more birds now than the puffin could count. A few, with added courage of companionship, had begun to venture a little nearer the mouth of the bay. The puffin waited, remaining with the main group, about a kilometre out. A buzzard joined his mate on the highest cliff, their mewing calls mixing with the persistent cries of mobbing gulls. The great birds ignored the mock attacks and the gulls lost interest, so that the only sound to reach the puffins was the dying echo of their calls from the dark cliff face. On the cliff top, the puffin respected the talon of the buzzard but, on the sea, he knew the safety of the water beneath.

While resting on the cliff edge, the puffins survey the ocean.

He was not as relaxed as he had been an hour ago; the day was steadily passing and the shadows were getting a little longer. The reason for his restlessness eluded him but he saw other puffins in courtship pairs and he felt lonely. The female he was expecting had not arrived. His feet no longer propelled him towards the island but began to paddle him towards one group of birds after another. Flicking his head at passing females, then billing with any that accepted his advances, he continued to move amongst the puffins in the quiet of the evening.

As the light faded from the sky, the puffin's interest in the island also waned. He wondered why he had moved so near the towering, black silhouette of the cliffs. They seemed cold and threatening and the open expanse of the ocean was so inviting. Three or four puffins nearby scuttered across

11

the surface of the water, smashing its calm into myriads of droplets. Instantly, the puffin felt almost a fear of the great black island and, with pounding heart, scrabbling feet and beating wings, he followed the little group out of the bay and into the ocean.

In the safety of the ocean's vastness, the puffin slept during the hours of darkness. If a puffin could dream, perhaps he relived the attraction, but mistrust, of the island, the pleasure of a beakful of fish and a chick underground, the excitement of companionship but the fear of the gulls. As the swell of the tide and the pull of the current carried the puffin throughout a night and a day, the island was gone from sight but not from his thoughts. Diving into the blue-green depths, the puffin saw only the empty ocean, a seemingly barren waste. Looking to his left, a small shoal of silver fish drifted across his field of vision but he had run out of air and was forced to surface. After a moment's refill of oxygen, he again slipped beneath the surface, excited in the pursuit of the fish. The small shoal was only a prelude to the huge shoal that filled the sea within minutes. The puffin dived and surfaced three or four times in quick succession. Swimming through the shoal of sparkling bodies, he grabbed and swallowed wherever he chose. His crop was now bulging but still he followed the shoal as if he could not bear to see such a feast depart. He had thoroughly gorged himself but the number of fish were not depleted and never would be, even if he gorged himself a hundred times over. Finally he allowed the fish to escape from his attention and shook his head to settle the meal in his crop.

During the morning, the puffin had followed the shoal, taking his fill whenever he chose. He had not seen another bird since leaving the island two nights previously but the excitement of the fish had taken him several kilometres east. A puffin flew overhead and again the island pulled at his thoughts; without a conscious decision, he found himself in pursuit over the ocean to the bay.

By mid-afternoon, the water beneath the cliffs was speckled with puffins, bobbing in the restless water. The stiff breeze had chivvied the water into a million choppy grey wavelets and the overcast sky drained the island of colour. Where the cliff protected the sea from the breeze, the water was still, almost like glass. A dark shape beneath the water drifted slowly towards a group of boulders which formed a temporary island at low tide. As the seal broke through the surface, the puffins gathered closer together, watching to see each other's reaction. The puffin arrived from the ocean, still with a bulging crop, and joined the group nearest to the seal. He watched the huge mammal nose amongst the seaweed around the boulder before heaving itself onto the miniature island. Paddling a few metres closer, the puffin allowed his curiosity to get the better of him for a moment or two then, losing interest in the creature, he spent the next hour preening with the rest of the colony.

Puffins were circling the cliffs above and a few were sitting on the grassy slopes, their white chests showing clearly amongst the sparse vegetation.

Huge rafts of puffins bob up and down on the waves.

Scuttering across the water, the puffins leave the bay.

12

Looking for a place to land.

To the puffins, who have spent the last 7 months at sea, the solid land feels strange beneath their feet.

Away to the west, the clouds began to break up, permitting the warm glow of the low sun to brighten the island. The number of birds on the nest slopes and in the air had increased over the past hour and the puffin was fascinated by the sight of the nest burrows that he had used for the past 6 years. He could not fly directly up to the colony because he was too close to the foot of the cliff and so he began his flight in the direction of the mouth of bay. Instead of keeping only a metre or two above the water, the puffin climbed higher and higher and then, turning into the wind, he aimed in the direction of the island. It was an exhilarating flight, a flight that he had not taken for 7 months.

The bay seemed larger and the atmosphere lighter than he remembered and there was a freedom in his flight. Banking steeply, he flew past his favourite landing spot outside the old burrow. He flew at speed with the wind behind him but he had no intention of landing. Turning towards the open water again, the bird swept away from the cliff, losing height as he used natural forces to gain speed. Diagonally across the bay he flew and, gaining height again, he approached the nest slope, this time into the wind. Using the wind and his bright orange feet as air brakes, he slowed a little, just over his favourite landing spot. At that moment, another puffin's head appeared from the entrance of his burrow. He repeated the circuit out over the bay, in a figure-of-eight formation. The other puffin was standing directly outside of the old burrow as he approached on the third circuit. Once

The puffins gather beneath the cliffs in the late afternoon and evening.

15

again, the puffin slowed down on the wind and, with a clumsy landing, settled on the very edge of the cliff.

For a full 2 minutes he simply stood where he had landed, barely moving, except for the occasional shuffle of webbed feet. He had not stood on his feet or touched any solid object since leaving the island last summer. All around, other birds were resting outside the burrows or pottering about the slopes. A fulmar petrel slid by on the updraught of air, on stiff wings but confident in its mastery of the air currents. On a protruding rock only a few metres away, five other puffins landed, one after the other. Their arrival reminded the puffin of its underground nest. When he had landed on the cliff edge, he was facing the sea but now he could see the dark, familiar burrow entrance. He took a few paces before stopping to look about for any signs of danger. He was rather edgy about being on land and was pleased to see that other puffins were quite relaxed. At last the puffin stood outside the burrow and turned to survey the scene that had been so familiar. He had bred in that burrow for five seasons now, although 2 years ago he and his mate had failed to raise a chick. He would never know that he had been raised in a burrow only 20 metres away but he knew the strong urge to return to that area.

A puffin approached him from a few metres away, a female who stumbled

As the evening light disappears, the puffins prepare to return to the sea.

on a loose pebble that shifted beneath her foot. Having regained her balance, she paused for a moment before nibbling a few white feathers into place. Once again she began to waddle towards the male and his burrow, picking her way more carefully between the tufts of plants. The male observed her approach and began to pad from one foot to the other, splaying out his feet to display their colour. He stood upright, with chest puffed out and chin tucked in, suddenly seeming confident in the environment of the cliff top and in the ownership of the burrow. The female was not deterred by his gestures and, with body held low and beak reaching forward, she walked quickly up to the male. Surprised by her blatant advance, he stumbled backwards but, instantly regaining his balance and dignity, they began to welcome each other in courtship. Although they had been separated for 7 months, they had reunited at their old burrow. They recognised each other now as if they had never been parted by the winter. They clashed their bills together in courtship, wagging them back and forth with such excitement that a group of spectator puffins gathered around. The last rays of the sun showed a colony full of puffins. A kindly face looked from the cottage window and grinned; the puffins had returned.

1 Description and Distribution

THERE are a few birds that have always had an extra appeal; a bird that catches your eye in a field guide and brings back fond memories or causes you to look forward to a future sighting. Perhaps it is the golden eagle or heron, maybe the kingfisher or peregrine falcon, but surely the puffin must fall into this category for most people. Perhaps it is the majesty of the eagle, the shape of the heron, the colour of the kingfisher or the drama of the peregrine which catches the imagination. The puffin, however, has an appeal all of its own, a friendly, comical character with a cheerfully-coloured beak. A visit to a puffin colony during the breeding months will guarantee close views of this very approachable bird. Every boatful of visitors to an island such as Skomer ripples with excitement at the first sight of this appealing bird. As the boat arrives at the island colony, fingers are pointed, cameras are loaded and enthusiasm abounds as puffins parade only a few metres away.

The puffin is a member of the auk family (Alcidae), which contains twenty-two species. The auk family includes guillemots, murrelets, auklets, the razorbill and, of course, the puffins. The auks are confined entirely to the northern hemisphere and, in the southern hemisphere, it is the penguin family that fulfils the same ecological niche. Although the auks and penguins are in no way related, their life styles are similar in many ways. As a result, their appearance is also similar; their legs are set well back on their body and their general shape is designed for life in the sea rather than on the land. On the whole, however, the auks have retained the ability to fly. Over 100 years ago, another species of auk, the great auk, fished the northern seas. Much larger than the other members of the family, it had lost the ability to fly and this was its final undoing. It was hunted by Man until the 1840s, when the last great auk was clubbed to death and the species became extinct. Of the twenty-two remaining species, six may be found in the North Atlantic: the common, Brunnich's and black guillemots, the little auk, razorbill and the Atlantic puffin.

The Atlantic or common puffin (*Fratercula arctica*) has several fairly close relations within the auk family, although it is the only puffin to be found in the North Atlantic. Closest is the horned puffin (*Fratercula corniculata*) of the northern North Pacific. A little larger than the common puffin, it is fairly similar in appearance except for a pair of rather strange horns of flesh that appear from just above the eyes. Other relations are the rhinoceros auklet (*Cerorhinca monocerata*) and the tufted puffin (*Lunda cirrhata*), which are also residents of the North Pacific, the tufted puffin is the largest of the group and, although it is mainly a dark-coloured bird, it has a long dramatic plume of a few yellow or white feathers extending behind each eye and drooping down to its back. The smaller rhinoceros auklet acquires its name from the large pointed horn at the base of its upper mandible. Although its beak is less conspicuous than that of other puffins, adornments include long white feathers behind the eyes and on both sides of its gape.

The puffin is well known as a stockily built, dumpy little character and is sometimes likened to a smart waiter wearing a dinner jacket and white shirt. When viewed on the land, in its breeding colonies, the bird stands about 200 millimetres high although, if measured from the tail to the tip of its beak, its overall length is 280–300 millimetres. It has a short, thick-set neck and its tail is very short and blunt. The whole of the bird's back is a glossy black although, after a tiring breeding season, the feathers lose their glossy appearance and may even look brown in colour as they become worn. The black area extends from the back to include the tail and wings, over the nape and crown and onto the forehead. A collar of black continues around the puffin's neck and joins across its throat. The whole of the underside (i.e. the front) of the puffin is white, including the undertail coverts, belly and breast. The areas of white, or rather light grey, which give a puffin that almost human character are the face patches. Covering the side of the face, these patches extend behind the bird's head in a gradually narrowing point which almost meets at the back of the puffin's head. The shape of the bird's head folds the plumage very slightly to the rear of the eye and this gives the appearance of a dark shadow extending towards the white point at the back of the head. It is this line or shadow which gives the sorrowful look to the puffin's eye.

The iris of the eye is very dark blue or brown and is surrounded by a noticeable red orbital ring. The eyes are exaggerated by two horny blue-grey patches of skin above and below the eye. The upper patch is roughly triangular while the patch below the eye is more rectangular.

Supporting the plump little bird are a pair of short, sturdy legs and large webbed feet. The legs are set far back on the body, giving the puffin its characteristic upright stance. Both the feet and legs are a

brilliant orange but the needle-sharp claws are jet black. It is interesting to note that the inner toe is twisted sideways except when in use; this is possibly to prevent the claw being blunted when standing on rocky nest slopes. The sharpness of the puffin's claws can be vouched for by anyone who has handled puffins, e.g. for ringing. Even the hands of experienced ringers become lacerated from the needle-sharp claws and, if a puffin can get a grip of a finger with its beak, the ensuing howls of pain give evidence to the power of its bite.

The puffin's beak must be one of its most appealing features. It is of course comically large and has been described as 'parrot-like'. The general shape of the beak, when viewed in profile, is triangular and bulky compared to the bird's size. Viewed from above or head on, however, the beak is quite slender and far more delicate-looking. The rather large and laterally-flattened bill is gaily coloured. Approximately half, nearest the tip, is bright glossy red-orange while the base area is a slaty blue-grey. These two areas are divided by a pale yellow ridge and the upper mandible is joined to the feathers by a pale yellow fleshy strip. At the join of the upper and lower mandible, a bright yellow, wrinkled rosette forms the corner of the gape.

When watching a colony of puffins, an experienced observer might detect a few slight variations to the above description of the beak. Differences in age and, to a lesser extent, sex are reflected in the beak

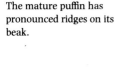

The mature puffin has
pronounced ridges on its
beak.

21

This puffin is less than 2 years old – it has a slim bill without any ridges.

and, in the winter months, even more interesting changes occur.

It is not until the bird is 4 or 5 years old that the puffin displays the beak of a fully mature bird. By the end of the first winter of the puffin's life, the beak will have reached its full length. However, it is still comparatively small and, over the next few breeding seasons, the bill will deepen and the top edge will curve upwards, so that the area of the beak becomes larger. A 1- or 2-year-old bird has a much more angular and pointed beak. As the beak develops in the immature bird, many show an upward kink on the top edge of the upper mandible, near the base. Each year, the colours become a little brighter and the markings even more pronounced. The eye embellishments also become a little larger each year, both the blue-grey patches and the red orbital ring. The main key to determining the approximate age of a puffin is the grooves that develop on the red portion of the beak. Both the upper and lower mandibles show these grooves as the bird develops. In general, the older the bird the more obvious the grooves become, and the more numerous. One-year-old puffins hardly show a groove at all on their beaks; 2-year-olds may show one, although it may be hard to see. By 3 years of age, one groove can easily be seen, and possibly even a second, and, by its fourth year, two grooves are completed. A few puffins may obtain a third groove in subsequent years.

A puffin that shows a single ridge on its beak is only 2 or 3 years old.

It is possible to determine the sex of a puffin from the size of its beak but the difference between male and female is not sufficient to allow this to be done visually. Measurements need to be taken of the length and depth of the beak and the surface area needs to be calculated. In general, male puffins have larger beaks but, unfortunately, the difference is not great enough to give a positive indication of the bird's sex every time. There is also a variation in bill size from one colony to another. One presumes that the size of the beak and its grooves indicate the sexual maturity of the birds to the other puffins. The feet and legs must also fall into this category as they too brighten with maturity.

A puffin in winter loses a little of its charm because, as its distinctive markings and colours fade, so does some of its character. The change is brought about in three ways. Firstly the decorated outer sheaths of the beak are shed, secondly the face of the bird becomes darker and, finally, the eye ornaments are lost. The tip of the beak remains largely unchanged but the blue-grey horny plates that cover the rear section are lost. The pale yellow strips that surround the horny plates also harden and eventually break away, leaving behind a much less conspicuous beak. The tip remains red, although not so bright, but the skin exposed beneath the outer sheaths is very dark. The beak appears smaller and is notched in at the top and curves up to the chin. Feathers behind the beak and around the eye become dark grey and the loss of the eye embellishments leaves the puffin's eyes looking small and fearful. This unfamiliar appearance is rarely observed because the birds are well out at sea during the winter months. On very rare occasions, the odd one in winter plumage may arrive at the breeding colony although the chances of it breeding are very slim. Each year, a few birds appear at a colony with dark feathering showing on their faces. However, to see a bird that is in almost full winter plumage is quite rare and it looks quite strange. Apart from the darkened face and less distinctive beak, I find the missing embellishment from the eyes to be the feature that most changes its appearance. It seems as if the eye adornments as much as the beak gives the puffin its character.

Very rarely, a 1-year-old bird may arrive at the colony.

Although we have seen that the puffin stands about 200 millimetres high, the actual size of the bird varies quite considerably throughout the breeding range. Puffins in the more southerly area tend to be smaller than those birds in the colder waters of the western and northern North Atlantic. For example, puffins from southern Britain have an average wing length of 158 millimetres and weigh on average 400 grams. A puffin from Spitzbergen would have an average wing length of 186 millimetres and might weigh over 50 per cent heavier – up to 650 grams. Due mainly to the difference in size and geographical distribution, the Atlantic puffin species (*Fratercula arctica*) is divided into three subspecies. The most northerly and largest subspecies is *naumanni* which breeds in northwest Greenland and Spitzbergen. Intermediate in size and the most widespread is *arctica* which is centred around Iceland but includes Norway, southwest Greenland, Canada and the USA in its range. The smallest subspecies, *grabae*, inhabits the British coast and southern Norway.

Even within a single colony there is a slight difference in size. The difference is mostly between the male and female birds, the males being about 9 per cent heavier on average than the females. It is frustrating that the small differences of size and beak do not enable the sex to be identified visually.

Dr Mike Harris, who is an international authority on puffins, permitted himself to speculate on the world population of this species. He felt that a figure of about 15 million birds would be as near as he could 'guestimate'. Assuming that figure to be correct, where are all these puffins to be found? As we have seen, they are confined to the North Atlantic and, because they are birds of colder waters, they are only rarely found south of the Mediterranean Sea. Even then the southerly trips are made only during the winter months. The true hub of puffin activities centres around Iceland, where there are more puffins breeding than in the rest of the world put together. Probably 60 per cent of all puffins nest around the coast of Iceland and, although much of the coast has colonies, perhaps some of the largest are on the Westman

Groups of puffins gather
on outcrops of rock at
the end of the day.

Islands to the south of Iceland. The coast of Norway also provides ideal nesting conditions for many hundreds of thousands of puffins. The majority of colonies, and the largest, are in the north, both on the mainland and on the many islands of the area. Røst is a collection of ten small islands and can boast the largest single colony in Norway, amounting to an estimated 700,000 pairs. It is truly difficult to visualise these colossal numbers of puffins, wheeling over the nest sites. Most of the islands making up The Faeroes complex have fairly large numbers of breeding puffins. The greatest population is on the small island of Mykines where more than 100,000 pairs rear their young each year. Puffins have also colonised the coasts of the USSR, Spitzbergen and Greenland but, in these locations, the colony size is measured in hundreds rather than thousands of pairs. The Channel Islands and the coast of France also support a few small colonies but, unfortunately, numbers have dramatically declined over the past hundred years. Now there is only a handful of colonies consisting of less than 100 birds at each site.

In the western Atlantic, there are many large and well-established sites. In excess of 330,000 pairs breed in over fifty different sites with the majority on the coast of Newfoundland, Canada. The Labrador coast also contains good-sized colonies. Further south, three islands off the coast of the USA have, in recent years, begun to re-establish puffin breeding sites.

Puffins often flutter their
wings whilst standing in
the colony.

These colonies were well established sites prior to the 1800s but shooting of puffins began around that time and the birds were exterminated from these islands. By 1887 there were no puffins on Machias Seal Island, which was the largest colony in Maine. On both the Western and Eastern Egg Rocks the puffins were shot until they also were wiped out in 1908. On Matinicus Rock a handful of puffins managed to survive but only one pair bred in 1902. The situation today is a credit to commonsense as well as legislation because, although the colonies may not be large compared with the more northerly colonies, Matinicus Rock has in excess of 125 pairs and Machias Seal Island has in excess of 1,000 breeding pairs.

Puffins were re-introduced to Eastern Egg Rock in recent years. Young chicks were taken from the thriving colony on Great Island off the Newfoundland coast. They were hand-reared and released on Eastern Egg Rock.

The successful re-introduction programme began in 1973 and since then over 700 puffins have been released. The young returned for several years and were encouraged to land by placing dummy puffins on the cliff tops. It was not until 1981 that 5 pairs were found raising young at the new colony, where today about a dozen pairs are established on Eastern Egg Rock.

Britain and Ireland support a fairly high population of breeding puffins, probably about a seventh of the world population. The majority of these birds nest on the coast and islands of Scotland but other smaller colonies can be found in many locations around England, Wales and Ireland. It would appear that the population associated with the British Isles has declined dramatically over the past century. There were many reports from the 1800s telling of colonies that were so immense that words could not adequately describe the experience of such huge numbers of puffins. Reports suggested 'a constantly moving, whirling, eddying, seething throng of life drifting and swooping, and swinging on the wind, or pitching and heaving on the water, or crowding and jostling on the ledges and rocks'. Others felt that 'the puffin has a complete hold over the whole upper crust', or 'their numbers seem so great as to cause a bewildering darkness'.

Even allowing for exaggerations and over-enthusiasm, many of these locations now have pitifully few puffins compared with a hundred years ago. However, other populations have expanded and probably the most dramatic is on the Isle of May in Scotland where, in 1959, there were only five pairs; today in excess of 10,000 pairs inhabit the island. The general trend (although numbers do not begin to compare with the last century) appears to be that over the past 10 years the puffin population has shown a significant increase of up to 25 per cent. Precise figures of population or colony size, and of any change within a large colony, are difficult to ascertain due to the variation in numbers of birds visiting the colony each day throughout the season. Also, because puffins nest underground, counting either birds or nests is hopelessly inaccurate. Careful work on many of Britain's major colonies has helped to build up an overall picture that suggests a possible 700,000 breeding pairs in Britain and Ireland, with over 600,000 of them established in Scotland or the Scottish isles.

Around the coast of Ireland, there are over thirty colonies but most of them are small, with only nine having over 1,000 pairs. It is the southwest of Ireland which holds the largest population, on the Kerry Islands. England and Wales have even fewer large colonies, with only five locations holding over 1,000 pairs. The Farne Islands, off the northeast coast of England, holds the largest population of 15,000–20,000 pairs. Further south in the North Sea, Coquet Island, Bempton and Flamborough Head also hold good numbers of puffins. No puffins nest further south, or along the south coast, with the exception of a few pairs on Portland Bill in Dorset and the nearby Purbeck cliffs. The west coast of England and Wales, is dotted with twenty-five or so puffin colonies; these are mainly small, many with less than 100 pairs. The exceptions to this are the two islands of Skomer and Skokholm off the southwest tip of Wales. Skomer has in excess of 7,500 pairs and is one of the most easily accessible puffin colonies.

The Scottish coast and its islands have by far the largest puffin populations in Britain. Colonies are scattered all around the coast and, excluding the Orkneys and Shetlands, account for over eighty individual sites. The largest numbers of puffins occur on the islands of St Kilda and Shiant and the largest mainland colony is at Clo Mor. These three sites together may account for 150,000–200,000 pairs. Other major sites include Sule Skerry, Dunnet Head, Mingulay, North Rona, Craigleith and the Isle of May. The high numbers of puffins breeding in the Orkneys and Shetland are made up of dozens of small colonies, many of which may consist of less than 100 pairs. However, at Hermaness in the extreme north, a very large colony of over 50,000 pairs exists. Foula provides the breeding ground for an even greater number and Fair Isle supports about 25,000 pairs.

The fact that puffins choose to nest either on islands or in remote areas with difficult access, gives an added excitement to anyone making the effort to observe them. A word of warning, however; many sites are located above high cliffs on steeply sloping ground. In a large colony, the whole area may be undermined by puffin nest-burrows and, as a result, the surface often becomes very unsafe. Added to this, on some locations, the burrows may be near the surface and a careless footstep could easily cave in the roof and crush the egg, chick or even an adult incubating bird. Several nesting areas are under the protection of a variety of conservation societies. As long as commonsense rules are adhered to, many societies encourage visitors and, in general, colonies such as these are the best places in which to observe the birds at close quarters. Puffins are amiable little creatures and, in colonies regularly visited by human beings, they will allow people to approach within a few metres, which is part of the pleasure of observing puffins. The fact that a view of maybe thousands of birds is guaranteed adds greatly to the anticipation of a boat trip to a puffin-inhabited island.

2 Life at Sea

A TYPICAL illustration of a puffin will probably show a bird standing at a breeding colony amongst many other puffins and a description of the puffin's environment will invariably include the rugged cliff tops, rocky outcrops, nest burrows and the sea as a backdrop. However, puffins do not live on cliff tops; they live in the vastness of the North Atlantic. They do, of course, visit the grassy slopes for the convenience of breeding but their lives revolve around the richness of the ocean. Many puffins do not return to land for 2 or even 3 years after they have taken their first plunge into the sea. Their shape, their colour and their behaviour is designed for life in the environment of the ocean. Disturb a bird on the cliff top and it will fly out to sea; frighten a bird off the water and it will not fly to the land, it will fly even further out to sea. The puffin feels safest on the water and is most at home in the ocean. It is a sea bird through and through.

The false impressions one gets of the puffin's life are hardly surprising because the bird is rarely seen kilometres out at sea. Research is almost impossible in the vastness of the ocean and, as a result, little is known of the puffin's life in that environment. During the winter months, or at least during the period of the year when the birds are not breeding, the puffin population is very widely dispersed from the breeding colonies. It is hard to imagine how such large numbers of distinctive birds can suddenly disappear, until one considers the size of the ocean. The population of puffins may be spread over 15–30 million square kilometres of sea, i.e. possibly 1 or 2 square kilometres for every bird. It is hardly surprising therefore that only six puffins were reported from 101 crossings of the Atlantic.

Once in the sea, the comical little character of the cliff top shows itself to be a very efficient master of its environment. On the surface of the water, it floats very buoyantly and appears broad-chested as it bobs about with the waves. Heavy seas rarely concern the puffin although, at times, the birds really do seem to be thrown about by the power of the waves. Beneath the water, the puffin's webbed feet are moving constantly; even when resting or apparently asleep, the paddling feet continue to manoeuvre the bird to face the wind. The legs and feet are situated well to the rear of the bird; experiments have shown this to be the most efficient position for propulsion through the water. Little orange feet paddling away in the vastness of the ocean seem to offer a rather ineffective method of locomotion. One would presume that, for long-distance movements, the bird would therefore fly; however, it is surprising to see how quickly the little bird is able to paddle around, even in a rough sea. We will see later how the young puffins leave the nest at night and, by sunrise, have paddled several kilometres out to sea. Also, I have observed puffins paddling out of a bay and along the coast. At the time, I wondered why the birds did not fly because it would have been so much quicker; nevertheless, I was still surprised to see how quickly the birds covered the distance. The bird moves steadily, drifting in the required direction and the movement appears almost effortless. This contrasts markedly with the puffin when it is in flight. The wings of a puffin are clearly a compromise between a useful flying device and an efficient underwater paddle. The result is that the wing area is overloaded and, to maintain flight, the bird has to beat its wings frantically at five to six beats per second. The effect is a vibrating, rather than flapping, wing beat in which the wings only travel through a short arc. Except at the breeding cliffs, the puffin rarely glides because the body-weight to wing-area ratio is too great. The inefficiency of its wings for flight is illustrated again when a puffin takes off from the water. The bird scuttles along the water surface, running on the water with its webbed feet whilst beating the air with its rapidly whirring wings. Once it has built up sufficient speed, it takes off, often assisted by a head wind. In a rough sea, the puffin may easily be caught by a high wave as it attempts to take off and, although at times it may look as if the puffin has met its end, it always bounces off the wave into the air or begins the take-off run again. Once in full flight, it usually stays within a metre or two of the sea. The puffin has a very direct flight and is surprisingly fast, easily capable of achieving speeds of 80 kilometres an hour and strong enough to fly into powerful headwinds. There is nothing graceful about a puffin landing on the water; it simply begins to lose height until it gets caught by the first wave, when it crashes into the wave in a most undignified fashion. In a calm sea, the puffin will lose height until only a few centimetres above the water and then it will simply stop flying; the resulting belly flop is as amusing as the 'wave crash'.

Overleaf: The true environment of the puffin is the open ocean. Puffins remain at sea all winter – far out in the North Atlantic.

Even in the most ordinary things the puffin is entertaining. The moment it lands on the water, the puffin plunges its head beneath the surface, peering into the depths. When I first saw this happen, I thought that the bird might be looking to see if any fish were present but, upon reflection, it seems more likely to be a safety precaution, in

31

case any predators are lurking beneath the surface. A great many sea birds have the same basic colour arrangement to the puffin, i.e. black upperparts and white underparts. It is generally considered that, in the expanse of the sea, where there is little protection from predators, this colouring is the most effective form of camouflage. Looking directly down from above the water, as an avian predator might do, the sea looks very dark and the black back of the puffin is therefore barely visible. On the other hand, when swimming beneath a group of puffins, if you look up towards the surface, the sky appears very bright and white and there can be little doubt that the white belly of the bird is at first quite difficult to observe. However, the brightly-coloured feet waving about like miniature semaphore flags are incredibly obvious. To a human being, they only look amusing but, to an underwater predator, they must be the signal for an easy meal. I shall never forget my first sight of a puffin from beneath the water: as I looked through my facemask the birds drifted closer, paddling along with their gaudy feet treading the water; then suddenly one comical face after another peered down at me from the surface. To me, they looked quite ridiculous and very funny, although I must have looked equally ridiculous to them because, in comparison with a human being, a puffin shows incredible agility under water.

The puffin's diet consists almost entirely of fish. Other food is taken on occasions but I believe that, given the choice, the puffin would live exclusively on fish. The contents of puffin's stomachs have been found to include pelagic worms and shrimps and a variety of crustaceans and molluscs. On occasions, these food items may be brought to nest colonies for young birds, possibly when the preferred fish are difficult to obtain. Many different fish may be taken; up to thirty-six species are on record as having been caught by puffins. However, some fish are clearly better value than others and the puffin appears to have the ability to select the fish that gives the best return for the effort of catching it. Some fish have a high oil content; others may contain relatively more water, and some species are far more abundant. The prey of the puffin most commonly includes sand-eels, herring and sprats and, further north and west, capelin becomes the main diet. All these fish have high calorific values and are abundant in the North Atlantic. The puffin has to be able to adapt to the fish that are available and the proportion of fish species in the diet may vary considerably throughout the season. The average length of the fish caught is about 70 millimetres but fish up to 180 millimetres can be dealt with, provided that they are long and thin rather than deep-bodied. A puffin probably needs to catch in excess of forty fish each day to survive, depending on the size of fish. This shows how efficiently the bird must function when under water.

A dive beneath the water may easily last up to 40 seconds,

A puffin plunges
beneath the waves,
using its wings as
paddles.

In underwater 'flight',
the puffin is
manoeuvrable and
graceful.

The puffin is able to dive
deeply in pursuit of fish.

although I have found 20–30 seconds to be the most common duration. In extreme situations, puffins can remain under water for over a minute. It would be inadequate to describe the puffin as 'swimming' under water because it uses its wings in a powerful, yet graceful, underwater 'flight'. Its wings are not fully extended and the primary feathers are held together so that the wings appear pointed. The bird becomes very streamlined as the water pressure holds its feathers tightly to its body and the air trapped in the feathers causes the puffin to shimmer with reflected light. When the bird first dives, a trail of air bubbles rises to the surface but, after a moment or two, the only bubbles to escape come from the bird's beak. The whole wing is used as a paddle under water; the feet are only used as a method of steering and not for propulsion at all. It is definitely more graceful and manoeuvrable under water than it is in the air and it can double back on itself very quickly in pursuit of a fish. The puffin pursues its prey by sight and is able to move its head in the increased water pressure because of the strong muscles of the neck. The wing bones of most birds are hollowed out, with air compartments for lightness, but the puffin (and the rest of the auk family) has solid wing bones to assist it in submerging. The wing bones are also flattened, which gives them a better angle of attack when 'flying' under the water. The puffin can move deceptively fast under water with a wing beat rate of up to two or three each second. However, quite often, each down stroke of the wings is followed by a long glide through the water, before the next wing beat. On these occasions, each wing beat may be 2 or even 3 seconds apart. Swimming beneath the water, the puffin may dive to a considerable depth. Puffins have been brought to the surface by trawlers gathering fish but it is difficult to be precise about the depth to which a puffin will dive. On one occasion, I was sitting under water at a depth of 10 metres and air bubbles were rising from my breathing apparatus in a silvery line. The puffins on the surface above me must have been fascinated by the stream of bubbles because they swam down the line of bubbles until they were only a metre away from me. They were clearly quite happy in 10 metres of water and could obviously go even deeper if required.

The aim of the puffin is to capture its prey just behind the gills but, if it catches the fish elsewhere, it is more than able to manoeuvre the fish into exactly the right position whilst still under water. Indeed, provided the fish is not too large it can actually be swallowed under water. Two or even three fish may be caught and swallowed in this way, all within the same dive. Larger fish, which are not so easy to deal with, are brought to the surface where they are swallowed whilst still wriggling. People often ask how a puffin is able to collect a whole beakful of fish and bring them back to the nest site for its youngsters. How can it hold one fish in its beak and then open it again to catch another? Does it catch the whole beakful in one dive or does it dive for each fish?

A puffin's beak has a very powerful grip and, as I have already mentioned, many ringers will vouch for this. It also has inward-facing serrations on the beak and a muscular grooved tongue. Its beak is therefore perfectly adapted to catch and hold a single fish. To hold a *row* of fish, a further adaptation allows the upper and lower mandibles to come together in a parallel fashion, so that the puffin can exert pressure equally along the whole length of its beak, not just in the narrow angle at the innermost end.

Having caught the first fish, the puffin is able to clamp it to the roof of its beak with its strong tongue and then open its bill again to catch the next item of prey. This is then clamped, by means of the tongue, alongside the first fish, and another fish can be pursued with an open beak. I doubt whether a whole beakful of fish can be caught in one dive so I presume that, having caught a few fish and run out of air, the bird surfaces. It then continues to dive until it has collected sufficient to make the flight home worthwhile.

To observe puffins at a feeding site is difficult enough but to be certain of what is going on is almost impossible. On one occasion I found a puffin on the surface of the water with no fish in its beak. After a few minutes of looking down into the water, it suddenly dived and remained under water for 28 seconds. When it reappeared, it carried at least three, and possibly four sand eels in its beak. After only 20 seconds, it dived again and remained under water for a further 22 seconds. This time, the number of fish were too difficult to count but I would guess at a total of six or seven. Two other puffins had flown into the area and three others were paddling in my direction. 'My' puffin dived again but the next bird to reappear had no fish at all. As one of the newcomers had disappeared, I guessed this was that bird. The bird I now believed to be 'mine' surfaced with fish in its beak, although it only carried about the same number as before. Other puffins had arrived by now and more birds began to surface with fish. Although I struggled to keep check on 'my' bird, it was impossible to be certain which bird was bouncing up from beneath the waves. I remained with the little group of puffins for some time and felt that perhaps eight or ten dives would fill the bird's beak ready for the flight back to the nest site. To be fair, this was only a guess and so many factors would affect the success of the birds. Examples of these variable factors include: species of fish, depth of shoal, density of shoal, size of fish, and distance from nest site. Bearing all these things in mind, I tend to simply enjoy my observations rather than draw too many conclusions from them.

Whilst the puffin is catching, and even swallowing, the fish under water, it cannot avoid taking in a quantity of salt water. It overcomes the problem of salt balance by its amazing ability to excrete salt from

its body either through its kidneys or, even more effectively, *via* special nasal salt glands.

One aspect of a bird's life that is often overlooked is the care and replacement of its feathers. It would probably be fair to say that the puffin spends over 2 hours a day in preening. This may include a long methodical preen, covering most of its body and taking perhaps 20 minutes, or simply a moment or two to scratch a few feathers into place that are uncomfortable or irritating. It is important that birds preen regularly for several reasons: to distribute oil which is obtained from the preen gland and keeps the feathers supple; to trap air between the feathers, thus insulating the birds from the cold of the ocean; to 'zip' together the feathers, particularly the flight feathers, so that in flight they act as one flexible unit; to keep the feathers clean because dirty feathers are not water repellent and a bird that spends most of its life on the sea cannot afford to allow water to reach its skin. If water were to penetrate the outer contour feathers and wet the soft down next to the skin, it would be impossible for the bird to dry itself again in the environment of the sea.

Preening whilst on the sea often begins with the puffin ducking its head under the water and flicking water over its back. It can preen

It is important for the puffin to preen in order to maintain the insulating properties of its feathers.

most of its feathers into place using its beak, although some parts of its anatomy are difficult to reach. The puffin rolls onto its side to expose the white feathers of its belly so it can preen them. The feathers of its head and neck are scratched into place with rapid movements of its foot.

Preening may also take place as a form of relaxation or as a displacement activity. A bird may have been frightened and be unsure what to do; rather than do nothing, it will preen violently for a few moments which may help it to forget the disturbance.

Feathers do not last for ever; they become worn and abraded, particularly during the breeding season and, as a result, need replacing each year. Most species of birds lose only one feather from each wing at a time and, once they have been replaced, another two are shed and replaced. This continues until the moult of the wings is completed. In this way, the bird is only reducing the effectiveness of its wings slightly and so is still able to fly. The puffin already has overloaded wings, as we have seen, and the loss of even one feather from each wing would make its flight even less efficient and involve a great deal of effort.

To avoid the extended moult period, the puffin moults all flight feathers simultaneously. Although this means that the moult is achieved quickly, there is the disadvantage of the bird becoming flightless for the period of the moult. This simultaneous moulting of the flight feathers is common to all members of the auk family as well as certain other species, e.g. ducks, geese and swans, all of whom become flightless at this stage. The inability to fly must make this one of the most difficult times of the puffin's year, particularly as the loss of feathers may also entail a reduction in the vital insulation from the elements. The moult of the body feathers follows the pattern of gradual loss and replacement seen in other species and so the body insulation is not adversely affected. In a flightless state, the puffin would be unable to escape from predators or the threat of oil on the sea. The moult takes place kilometres out at sea during the winter or the early spring months. Most puffins are flightless between January and March, and first-year birds probably a month or two later. This means that adults will return to the nest site, with new flight feathers, at just the time of year when they will fly the most. When the puffin has lost its main feathers, the area of the wing normally used in flight is reduced by 40 per cent. For underwater movement, however, the wing is still almost as efficient and, when bent for swimming, it retains over 80 per cent of its original area. Once again this illustrates what an efficient bird of the ocean the puffin is.

Any research into establishing where puffins spend the winter, or indeed where they are when the nest slopes are deserted, has always been very difficult. Two obvious major problems make the task of being specific about the puffin's winter location nearly impossible:

Throughout most of its life, the puffin roosts on the water.

firstly the very low numbers of ringed puffins that are found and, secondly, the area of sea that is involved. Over a period of years, tens of thousands of puffins have been ringed yet, for every 1,000 birds individually identified in this way, only seven are ever recovered away from the nest area. This is a recovery rate of only 0.7 per cent and that is much lower than for most other birds. Most of the puffins that are recovered have been found either washed ashore (about 25 per cent of these are oiled), shot or caught in fishing nets. Although information gained from these birds is very interesting and useful, it is undoubtedly biased and should be interpreted with great care. The fact that the majority of recoveries are from birds washed onto the beaches gives the impression that puffins overwinter just off the coast. Of course, it is only the washed-up birds which are found; the ones that die hundreds of kilometres out at sea sink out of sight. In some countries, puffins used to be shot regularly and some birds were recovered in this way; when the shooting stopped, puffin recoveries ceased so statistically it looked as if puffins no longer visited the areas in question. Similarly, if we consider a particular area favoured by fishermen who bring in several puffin recoveries from their nets. The weight of recoveries may seem to favour that area as a popular winter location for puffins. Or it

By ringing puffins and marking burrows, researchers are able to trace puffin movements.

may indicate that other areas are not fished so heavily! Ornithologists who are involved in collating the information gathered from ringed birds are well aware of these problems and so only a very general guide can be given. The very low recovery rate (0.7 per cent) away from the nest area probably indicates that puffins winter even further out to sea than other auks. A comparable rate for other auks ringed in Britain is 2.5–3 per cent. Most puffins winter out on the open sea and when they die they sink and so do not help bird enthusiasts answer their questions. Various efforts have been made to monitor bird numbers in the North Atlantic as well as in the North Sea. Records have been kept regularly of sightings from oil platforms and a variety of ships in the area. The size of the ocean seems to overwhelm the possibility of gathering any really useful information and I have already suggested that 1 or 2 square kilometres is available for each puffin. About 800 ringed puffins have been recovered away from the nest site and the general impression gained from these birds is that puffins ringed in colonies on the coast of eastern Britain and southern Norway remain in the North Sea and English Channel. They do not in general go far west into the North Atlantic. It is the birds from western Britain and Iceland that seem to travel further, covering the North

41

Atlantic, including the Bay of Biscay and even into the Mediterranean Sea. Birds from western Britain have been found as far south as Morocco and the Canary Islands, as far west as Canada, and into the Mediterranean Sea as far as Sicily. These were mainly first-year birds which do travel more widely and are the extreme cases. Many birds will not travel this far and much of their movements at sea are still a mystery.

It is difficult to visualise the conditions which the puffin faces during some of the winter months. From the small amount of evidence available to date, it appears that the puffin is a solitary bird throughout the winter months, but it is difficult to imagine a bird which is so gregarious at the nest site spending the whole of the winter alone on the sea. Therefore it is easier to believe that small, loosely-attached groups of birds spend at least a little time together in the winter, constantly separated by waves and darkness yet remaining in the same general area. However, there is no evidence to establish whether or not this is the case. It seems that, for most of the winter, the puffin is very much alone, perhaps spending much of its time resting on the water with howling winds above and heaving sea beneath.

One can imagine the bird being lifted to the crest of the wave and the wind beginning to cut through it's feathers. The puffin would hurriedly paddle its feet to face the onslaught of the biting wind, while spray was caught on the wind and hurled into it, forcing it to close its eyes. Only seconds later it would be lowered by the sea and protected from the wind by the same wave that had lifted it into the wind's full force. The rise and fall of each wave would be echoed in the sound of the wind, a world of constant movement and noise. I would imagine that, beneath the waves, as the bird dived deeply, there would be a sudden peace, a calm that contrasted with the air above. Perhaps at times it would seem warmer beneath the waves. On other occasions, when hungry and tired the puffin might find the underwater world to be empty and barren, an endless cold green waste, until a shoal of fish appeared. On the surface again, the puffin might try to stay in the troughs of the waves for protection and to wait for the sea to settle. After all, if the bird were moulting, it would be flightless and unable to go far. Heavy cloud cover would make the night very dark and then the puffin would not even be able to see which wave was moving it. The bird could only feel the ocean's movements in its body and correct its course with its feet. Driving rain and sleet would eventually give way to a calmer day when the waves would subside. The puffin could see again because its vision would not be obstructed by tower blocks of moving water. Perhaps it could then see, or rather sense, where it was, despite the hundreds of kilometres of water in all directions. In contrast to the howling gale, a peaceful day at sea must be incredibly silent.

42

After 7 months at sea, the puffin lands near the island colony.

In the previous paragraph, I hope that I have put together a taste of the conditions at sea in winter. I appreciate that puffins do not have human thoughts or feelings and therefore the sea may appear very different to them. However, I believe that to relate to a bird one must relate to the bird's environment and, in this chapter, we have seen that the puffin's environment is not the summer cliff tops but the ocean.

3 The Puffin Colony

THE puffin is an efficient little bird and would be quite capable of breeding on its own in a secluded part of the coast. However, it has given up its individuality and has become only one of a large number of puffins that form the puffin colony. The colony appears to act as a single unit, constantly relying on its members' movements. Communication is by signal and sight and each bird is interested in its neighbour. Because puffins rely on the visual sense, the entire colony can be divided into sub-colonies, i.e. those birds that can see each other. The dividing line between these groups is often a physical barrier, e.g. high bracken cover or an area that is not suitable for burrowing. In many situations when I refer to the colony it would be more accurate to use the term sub-colony.

The preferred location for a colony is a remote and secluded situation, therefore the largest numbers of colonies are on islands. The main feature about many island sites is that ground predators are absent. The puffin finds it difficult to be successful where such predators are abundant.

All sides of an island will be used where the habitat is suitable. The majority of puffins nest underground in burrows, therefore the soil type must be suitable for digging. If a puffin is able to take over a rabbit burrow, it will readily do so and a great many colonies are based on the efforts of rabbits. A rabbit can be given a very nasty peck to force it to leave its surface runs and, with only a small amount of digging, the puffin will have the burrow to its liking and will take over completely. In a few locations, puffins nest in crevices amongst rocks and boulders but, apart from this slightly different nest site, the puffins behave in the same way.

The hub of the colony revolves around the steep grassy slopes, often just above the cliffs. These prime nest locations are much sought after because they have an easy approach but, more importantly, the line of escape to sea is very direct. Puffins find it difficult to take off on level ground. They have to scramble across the vegetation until they gain

A group of puffins rest on a lichen-covered rock.

Puffins inspecting nest burrows near the edge of the cliff.

45

enough speed to become airborne. A direct drop nearby, or at least a slope, is a great advantage when fleeing to safety so it is always the slopes that are the first to be colonised. As the colony expands, however, the flatter ground will become riddled with burrows. Another factor limiting the development of the colony is the vegetation. Young birds joining the colony after several years at sea feel vulnerable and insecure when on the land. When they first arrive at the colony, and as they first investigate the cliff tops for a suitable burrow or nest location, they continually refer to the adults for reassurance and guidance. Because they need to be constantly in visual contact with other puffins, these sub-adults rarely land or wander into tall vegetation. Once the vegetation blocks their view of other puffins, they panic, assuming it to be unsafe. Probably the most common plant to limit the expansion of puffin colonies in this way is bracken, which is prolific in the cliff-top environment. Although the bracken does not begin to grow until well into the breeding season, the prolific leafy growth coincides with the later arrival of the younger birds in June and July. I have found, through the years, that by removing the bracken at the critical time, when youngsters are looking for nest locations, the colony is able to expand. However, tall vegetation does not prevent an established pair from nesting successfully and they will continue to feed their chick as the plants grow around them.

A puffin relaxes near the edge of the cliff.

In the evening puffins gather on the cliff top.

What are the chances of a new colony beginning? Puffins have an extremely strong loyalty to the colony where they were raised. They also need to see that other puffins are present before they will even land to look for nest sites. As a result, the chances of a new colony forming are extremely slim. Indeed a great many traditional locations have been deserted over the years but there are only one or two reports of colonies being established. One of these locations is the Eastern Egg Rock situated off the northeast coast of the USA. As a result of Man's persecution, the island was deserted by puffins for 70 years. A deliberate effort was made to re-introduce them and, after 7 years, about a dozen pairs are now established at that site. In Scotland, other sites which could be classed as re-established are found on the Isle of May and other islands in the Firth of Forth. In 1958, only five pairs of puffins were breeding on the Isle of May and, today, about 10,000 pairs breed there. Two smaller islands nearby also have in excess of 1,000 puffins whereas, only 12 years ago, there were no puffins at all breeding on these islands. It would appear, from the results of ringing, that a large number of these puffins arrived from the nearby Farne Island where the birds had dug parts of the island almost to destruction.

The digging activities of puffins can eventually force them to desert a long-established colony. The effect of a high density of puffins, all

47

improving and extending their burrows, is to undermine the layer of
top soil. As burrows intermingle, cross and converge beneath the
ground, the whole upper surface becomes unstable until eventually it
may collapse. Many colonies are dug into light sandy soils or soils that
are high in organic matter. They are particularly prone to collapse
near the entrance or on level ground when the roof of the burrow is
not far beneath the surface. Partly as the result of the burrows, the top
soil becomes extremely dry in the heat of summer and vegetation is
unable to thrive. In this unstable condition, the soil is eroded from
above by the wind. It is also removed from beneath by thousands of
puffins digging, as they repair the deteriorating burrows. Two locations that illustrate this type of destruction are the Farne Islands and
the Island of Grassholm; the latter now retains no breeding puffins as
a result.

The puffin is very loyal to its own colony, the adults returning year
after year to the same burrow and the majority of youngsters returning to their parent colony to nest. However, it is not uncommon for
juveniles and, to a lesser extent, adult puffins, to visit other nearby
islands that have puffins in residence. Quite why they choose to visit
another colony is not certain because it is unusual for them to remain

A puffin prepares to
drop into the colony.

48

to breed, although this does occasionally happen. It illustrates the birds' eagerness to be with other puffins in the spring and summer months when the attraction of the colony is very strong.

Clearly there are advantages as well as disadvantages in the puffin giving up its individual identity and becoming part of a large number. The disadvantages, however, appear to be few, with only one major problem. Finding a suitable burrow or selecting a site to commence digging is not easy for a young puffin returning to the colony. By the time the sub-adults arrive, the best locations will already be occupied by the breeding adults. The adults can easily defend their burrows from the inquisitive sub-adults by demonstrating their maturity with a dignified upright posture. On the odd occasion, a disrespectful youngster may even deserve a peck to keep it in order. It is not by chance that sub-adults arrive at the colony once the breeding birds are well into the season. It prevents any serious competition for burrows occurring at a time when the breeding population is settling in. This means the breeding birds can simply return to their old burrows, which have been selected and prepared in the previous seasons, and immediately begin lining the nest and egg-laying. When the sub-adults join the colony, from May onwards, they struggle to fit in amongst the other birds or to establish a site on the edge of the colony. In this way, order is kept within the colony and fighting is kept to a minimum.

There are several advantages to nesting in a colony and, although at times it may be difficult to find a nest site when a colony is crowded, it is easy to find a mate. There seems to be no attempt to attract a mate to a new nest site. A puffin simply investigates the site and a member of the opposite sex that is also looking for a location agrees on its suitability. The pair bond is initially formed by the attachment to, and the defence of, the burrow. The unity of the pair develops throughout the season as they are together at the burrow, billing together, digging together, resting together and defending the burrow together. A burrow owner has no problems finding a mate. It is very difficult to determine whether either of the pair takes a dominant role in the protection of the burrow or the establishment of the pair bond. I have seen both male and female birds displaying ownership and even using physical force. It would also appear the both birds are equally eager to begin courtship billing.

The idea that there is security in numbers seems to be well illustrated within the puffin colony. There are hundreds or thousands of eyes looking for any signs of danger and one or two birds leaving the clifftop in fright can panic a large part of the colony. Once disturbed in this way, the birds will fly in a huge circuit across the cliffs and out over the ocean, returning over the cliffs to repeat the circuit time and again. A few birds regain the courage to settle on the cliff tops and

these are promptly followed by the rest of the colony on the next circuit. As groups of birds are disturbed from different parts of the colony, and as birds are arriving from the ocean, the sky becomes filled with birds wheeling around in a huge circuit. These circling birds are often described as being in 'wheels'. The wheels appear to be more noticeable in some colonies than others but, where they occur, they are always exciting to observe. The reason for the wheel is connected with the wind direction and with the puffin's cautious nature. A puffin likes to fly over its proposed landing area a few times before it finally settles. If other puffins are present, indicating that it is safe to land, then it may only fly past once or twice. If on the other hand there are no other puffins settled nearby, then the puffin may fly over ten or more times. A puffin's approach to the land is always into the wind, as near as is possible, and it will fly with the wind as it leaves the cliff top. The need to land into the wind conveniently means that the birds will all fly in the same direction, thus preventing any head-on collisions. It has been suggested that these wheels are display flights and have many useful purposes. However, from my own observations, I would describe them as reconnaissance flights in which the wind direction largely controls the direction of the wheel. One evening, I was watching puffins wheel over the cliff tops just as the sun was setting; the birds were coming up over the slopes to my right, flying past me and dropping away to the sea on my left. The following evening, I went to watch the sun set at exactly the same location and I realised that the puffins had reversed the wheel and were now arriving on my left and, having flown past me, were departing on my right. The only reason for this I could find at the time was that the wind direction had changed.

Whether the puffins benefit from wheeling is hard to assess. It has been suggested that large numbers of birds circling around confuses predators and I have shared this feeling when trying to photograph puffins in flight. The more birds that were flying past, the more distracted I became by the following birds. I always felt that the next puffin would be easier to photograph than the one I was following with my camera and, as a result, I missed both. This may also apply to a predator or a gull that is on the lookout for a chance to steal a puffin's fish (see Chapter 6). Certainly a predator prefers to select a lonely bird. Careful observation will show that the wheels increase as sub-adults join the colony and they occur in the evening when more sub-adults are coming into land. It is these less-confident birds that may spend time circling the colony. Adults actually arriving with fish or leaving the colony do not circle for long. I feel that, if a wheel is formed, it is either the result of a panic or is a flight of convenience or reconnaissance for birds joining or leaving the colony. Any benefits gained by avoiding predators are a bonus.

In general, puffins that nest in the most dense part of the colony suffer the least predation. If the population of predators is high then it is possible for as many as 4 per cent of puffins on the outskirts of a colony to be killed, compared with only 1 per cent in the centre. The effect of the higher mortality figure will be shown in Chapter 6. Clearly the advantages of nesting in dense colonies outweigh the disadvantages.

On landing, the bird leans forward with wings held open as a submissive posture.

Wherever any species of bird is breeding in close proximity to one another, there are certain to be disputes. With the puffin, arguments are mainly over nest burrows but surprisingly little physical contact takes place. However, on occasions, quite dramatic fights do break out, as we will see. The puffins convey to each other information which could be described as peace-keeping, social behaviour. When observing puffins on the cliff tops, it becomes apparent after a time that there are different methods of walking about the colony. Birds flick their heads or open their beaks for no obvious reason and there are little routines which they observe when taking off or landing. The reason for some of these activities is clear but for others is uncertain.

When the puffin arrives at the nest site, it may land amongst dozens of other puffins. At the moment of landing, it is probably not sure who its immediate neighbours are and does not want to upset them. Therefore the puffin leans forward with its body horizontal and low to the

A low crouching run demonstrates the puffin's passiveness.

ground. The head is held forward but kept low and usually one foot is placed well in front of the other. Most noticeable is the fact that the puffin does not immediately close its wings but holds them half open for a moment. This is the landing posture and is an appeasement posture to prevent it being attacked by the other puffins which it has joined. In general, low postures can be associated with submissiveness or appeasement. Some individuals will still display this posture, even when no other birds are present but, in general, it becomes exaggerated when a puffin lands amongst a dense group.

The low posture that demonstrates submissiveness comes into operation again as puffins move about the colony. A puffin that lands on the cliff edge may need to move through the colony to find its own nest burrow. It is interesting to watch the puffins move past other nest entrances and to observe the interaction between the birds. The bird that is simply passing through keeps its profile low by holding its body in a horizontal position, with its head down and back rather hunched. It will scurry past an occupied burrow quite quickly and, once past, may stand up straight for a moment or two to have a look around. It continues its journey with low-posture runs punctuated with a few seconds observation to make sure there is no danger. The burrow owner usually ignores the passing bird, declaring its site ownership simply by its confident presence outside the burrow.

Overleaf: A puffin gapes to demonstrate its dominance.

With exaggerated footsteps, the puffin parades like a clockwork toy.

A puffin may also attempt to declare ownership of a burrow in a variety of movements or displays that illustrate its maturity or dominance. These little displays, which are most amusing to watch, in general exaggerate either the birds' size or its beak. Although most of the dominant gestures are concerned with burrow ownership, they may also be used when the birds gather to rest on the cliff tops in the evening. I have seen a resting bird get up and move away to allow a dominant bird to take its place on a favourite cushion of thrift. As soon as it leaves and the thrift becomes vacant, the first bird will move back to settle down again.   On one occasion the dominant bird disturbed the other puffin three times in only 15 minutes. As I watched, it seemed as if it was behaving in this way simply to be a nuisance or to assert its dominance. The three main gestures which indicate a puffin's intention of asserting its dominance are head jerking, gaping and a rather upright, proud walk. It is the upright walk, which gives the bird a larger and bolder appearance, that is used most often. The puffin stands virtually upright with its tail cocked out and the beak held down so that it rests on its puffed-up chest feathers. As the puffin walks, each step is exaggerated and each foot seems to be deliberately placed, almost in slow motion. The effect of this walk is to give a bobbing movement as the puffin moves along. It is not always neces- sary for the puffin to walk in order to perform this motion because birds will display in this way whilst standing outside the burrow. Instead of walking, the puffin simply pads its feet up and down on the spot, rather like a soldier marking time. The webs of the feet are deliberately splayed out so it is possible that the bird is displaying the colour of its feet as a sign of maturity.

I saw a puffin approach another on the edge of a sheer cliff where they were resting. As it approached, it became more upright with chin tucked in and chest puffed out. It walked right up to the other puffin and, using its chest as a buffer, pushed the bird right off the cliff edge. The defeated puffin flew away and the victor opened its beak wide for a second in a gaping gesture.

Gaping can become a positive threat gesture; it may be used briefly to a passing bird or can build up into a battle of personalities. Generally, it is merely a warning but, on occasions, two puffins may face each other with their beaks held wide open, their tongues showing and their neck feathers erected. Although the adversaries are facing each other, they will turn their heads to one side to show their profile to each other. It has been suggested that this is to avoid direct eye contact, which may stimulate physical aggression, but I feel it is also probable that the birds are attempting to show their beaks to the best advantage. Their beaks, as we have seen, indicate their maturity and possibly their status in the colony.

Head jerking is very similar to head flicking during courtship. The head movement is roughly the same, although rarely so exaggerated, and each jerk is a second or two apart rather than a continuous movement. The bird usually stands upright and looks tall and slender during head jerking. I have always found it a difficult behaviour to explain; on each occasion when it is used it appears to mean something different. At times I would definitely associate head jerking with dominance because I have seen it coupled with other aggressive attitudes. A sub-adult puffin which was inspecting burrows looking for a vacant site was surprised by an adult bird appearing out of the hole. The youngster retreated rapidly and the owner came out to stand beside the entrance, where it jerked its head two or three times before it gaped. This was one of several incidents that gave me the impression that head jerking was connected with dominance. Head jerking must draw attention to the puffin's beak in the same way as courtship head flicking. It, therefore, seems reasonable to assume that it draws attention to the puffin's maturity and possible dominance.

Puffins will resort to physical violence to settle a dispute; a sub-adult that has become too inquisitive will be put into place with a sharp peck. It is not uncommon to see puffins fighting, although, bearing in mind the numbers of puffins that may be present in the colony, fights are a surprisingly rare occurrence. However, when two birds do become entangled in a battle, it can be both vicious and

prolonged. It would seem that most battles commence over the ownership of a burrow and, although the fight may begin on the cliff top, it may continue well out to sea. Other puffins gather around the scrapping pair, like schoolboys watching a fight in the playground. I have never seen the actual start of a fight, each time, my attention has been caught the moment after the fight commenced. The adversaries face each other with their neck feathers raised and with wings drooping forward and held away from their body. Both birds hold their beaks open wide in a gape display but, on this occasion, it is obvious that the gape is a prelude to vicious pecking. As the birds leap towards each other, they attempt to bite any part of the adversary's anatomy – commonly the neck or wings – or the beaks interlock. If one puffin manages to get a good grip, then the battle consists of the other bird trying to break free. The birds flap and struggle, trying to maintain balance using their wings. Often they tumble one over the other, down the cliff and, on one occasion which stands out in my mind, the assailants fell over the cliff and became lodged in some thick ivy that grew about 10 metres from the top. They continued to fight whilst suspended in the ivy at least 15 metres above the sea, their struggles sending a shower of leaves fluttering down. Eventually the pair, still

As the puffins fight in the sea, water droplets and feathers fly.

58

interlocked, fell from the ivy and hit the rocks beneath. Separated by the impact, they bounced in different directions and both tumbled into the sea just beneath the cliff. To my surprise, they had not forgotten their grievances and immediately began to face up to each other again on the water. Their tails were low in the water as they floated with chests high. Gaping as before, except now a breathless panting seemed to accompany the opened beaks, they lunged towards each other again, almost leaping clear of the water, seeming to lock beaks and twisting this way and that with their heads. Bright orange feet were used to scratch each other as they thrashed about in the water for minutes at a time. After a rest and a bout of gaping whilst facing each other, the fight continued. I then began to notice that one bird seemed to be more intent on fighting whilst the other was more intent on escape. The latter did not attempt to fly away but, as it was pursued, turned to face its adversary and fight again. It then dived beneath the surface, pursued by the other puffin. I was amazed to see that, when they came up, they shot at least half a metre clear of the water and were locked together in combat again. This happened on three other occasions and, each time they appeared from beneath the water, they were fighting. Twenty-five minutes after the fight first began on the cliffs, the escaping bird flew off across the water, to land about 80 metres away. To my amazement, it then began to paddle back across the water and, within 5 minutes, the pair were fighting again. Their flapping struggles took them further and further out to sea, until I needed binoculars to see them. They must have continued the fight for at least another 15 minutes before their anger subsided. The total length of the fight was nearly three-quarters of an hour. It is surprising that fighting puffins rarely cause each other physical damage. This, and many other puffin fights that I have watched, illustrated to me the importance that puffins place on burrow ownership and how essential peace-keeping social behaviour is for the effective working of the colony. Some birds have been so engrossed in their conflict that I have been able to approach to within a metre of them and, on one occasion, could almost reach out of a small boat to touch them. They would therefore be very vulnerable to predators.

For most of the time, the puffin colony is a very peaceful place. The apparent hive of activity is deceptive when you look more closely. During the first few hours of daylight, the adults are the only birds present at the colony, arriving with fish for the chicks underground and then leaving for the ocean again. Only a few puffins are at the colony during the morning and early afternoon and these birds will be resting on the slopes around the colony or on the water. During the afternoon, numbers begin to build up as the adults arrive, some with fish for their offspring. Having fed the chick, they do not rush back to sea but rest on the island with the growing numbers of other puffins.

The gusting wind causes problems to a puffin landing with fish.

Preening is a very important part of every puffin's day.

The puffin pinches its preen gland to obtain a supply of oil.

Wing feathers are nibbled into place during preening.

Head feathers are scratched into place using a webbed foot.

Beneath the cliffs, the water is dotted with hundreds of resting birds, many of them sub-adults which also join the colony during the late afternoon. There appears to be a lot of activity by early evening and birds seem to be constantly flying past but, as you look around, the majority of the birds on the grassy slopes are simply resting outside their burrows. Many of them may spend half an hour preening and some of the younger birds may try their hands at a little mild flirtation. In fact, many youngsters may crowd together on a favourite rock near the colony, where they can become accustomed to the feel of solid land beneath their feet and share the close company of other puffins. There are always birds on the water and a few scutter across the surface, leaving a wake of white water as they take off to circle the colony. Perhaps they will fly around three or four times before landing. Some adults will join the circling birds and land with a beakful of fish and a few others will leave the cliff and settle on the water to preen with a great deal of splashing. As a human observer watches the colony, one's eyes follow the points of activity, maybe some juveniles in courtship billing or a fish-carrying bird flying past. However, the majority of birds will be doing very little as they rest until the sun is set. At the last light, the whole colony will leave in a colossal wheel to fly out to sea.

The puffins roost on the water, probably close to the fishing

The puffin is able to hold a large number of fish in its beak.

Before taking off, the puffin signals its intentions.

grounds. They do not seem to be interested in the companionship of the other puffins whilst at sea and they will be dotted over a large area. The advantage of spending the night at sea is that they are in the best fishing areas at first light. In the most northerly colonies, the puffins are able to see to catch fish for almost 24 hours.

One puffin suddenly taking off from the colony will startle other nearby birds into a panic flight which may unsettle the whole colony. To overcome this problem, a bird that decides to leave the cliff top indicates its intentions by slightly exaggerating its pre-flight preparations. Bending its legs to lower its body into a horizontal position, the puffin opens its wings a little. Having displayed its intention for only a second, the puffin then launches itself into its quivering flight down to the sea. The flight that the puffin uses to leave the nest site is unusual. It has been described in several publications and many people have associated it with a courtship flight. In my opinion it is not connected with courtship at all but is a method of losing height quickly without stalling in mid-air. The head of the puffin reaches forward and down, giving a hunch-backed appearance. The feet are held tightly together, or are even crossed on occasions and the wings are held high above the body vibrating in a very short arc. The reason for the unusual flight is because the puffin's aim is to lose height as quickly as possible to get to the sea. The puffin is not designed for efficient flight and needs

63

to counter the effects of gravity and its movement through the air with rapid short wing beats. The bird's crossed feet cut down wind resistance because the tendency is for the bird to either stall on the up current or topple forwards. Watching the birds leaving the cliff top, one can almost sense the delicacy of the operation; it is certainly not a relaxed flight. I have spent many hours watching puffins leaving the cliffs in an attempt to determine whether or not this is a courtship flight. My own observations have shown that this flight is used throughout the day, when many birds are present and when there are no other puffins to display to. Throughout the season, all ages and sexes of birds left the cliffs in this way and, even when I disturbed the resting puffins from the slopes, they would fly with quivering wings, legs crossed and backs hunched. I found that one of the best ways to photograph this flight was to wait for a gull to panic a group on the slope above me and to capture the hunched effect and crossed feet as they flew past. If the puffins fly in this way even when frightened, I find it hard to conclude that it is a courtship flight.

Partly as the result of an inborn understanding and partly through their inquisitive nature, the sub-adults learn to adapt to the behavioural language of the colony. The sub-adults have survived their learning period at sea and, when they join the colony, they must learn from the older birds about life on land. By the time the sub-adults arrive at the colony, the older birds' plumage is slightly abraded and dull. The younger birds stand out with their glossy black backs and smaller beaks. They constantly look to the adults for guidance, not only with regard to safety but also in connection with breeding behaviour. I have seen an adult bird tugging at a clump of sea campion and disappearing down the burrow with a few strands in its beak. Immediately, a sub-adult rushed over to the plant and began to peck at the leaves. Having picked up a stem, it stood for several minutes with the plant in its beak, looking about with a mixture of pride and stupidity. Not knowing what to do with the leaf, the puffin allowed the wind to blow it away. If one bird flutters its feathers into place, having just landed, another bird may copy it. If one puffin flicks its head, a youngster may do likewise. The sub-adult may suffer as a result of its inquisitive nature. I have seen several attempts to follow an adult down a burrow and the youngster getting a peck for its trouble. A few sub-adults have even arrived at the colony with fish-laden beaks. Because they have no chick to feed, they eventually may attempt to eat them, but many are dropped on the ground and nearby puffins rush over to pick them up before the gulls snatch them away. Sometimes a young bird edges towards an adult that has a beakful of fish and tries to steal one from its grasp. The adult will then display its dominance and may even call in annoyance.

The puffin's low, soft, growling call, *arr-arr* is difficult to explain.

Sometimes it is clearly associated with aggression whilst, on the water early in the season, it seems to be associated more with courtship. Possibly, therefore, it somehow illustrates maturity and can be used in both situations. Maybe there is a greater variation in sounds than the human listener can hear, but even tape recordings played back to puffins have failed to get a response that we can monitor. In comparison with most bird colonies, the puffin colony is extremely quiet. However, the soft growls can be heard throughout the season in a great variety of circumstances, including underground in the burrows. I have never heard any satisfactory explanations with regard to puffin sounds and I am not about to reveal any more of the mystery that the puffin keeps from us. I sometimes wonder if puffins know what their calls mean; other puffins seem to ignore them!

All the activities of the colony are greatest during the evening and this is clearly the best time to sit and enjoy puffins. Very quickly the behaviour of the colony which I have outlined in this chapter, will begin to absorb the observer. But the purpose of all the activity is beneath the ground. It is the aim of each bird to work together to raise a chick. The adults are intent on this year's chick, while the sub-adults are finding burrows and mates for future years – and future generations.

4 Courtship and Egg-Laying

HAVING been at sea for about 7 months, the puffins begin to return to the colony. As the day length increases and the sea begins to warm up, the puffins start their journey back to the coasts of the Atlantic Ocean. The instincts deep within the birds draw them, not only to the island on which they bred in the previous season but to the very same burrows.

From the middle of March, I begin to watch for the first arrivals, wondering if they will turn up this year. I know that they will, they always do, but I cannot help looking for them.

Small rafts of puffins, maybe twenty birds in all, gather on the water a kilometre or two off the coast. The time of the puffin's arrival offshore is well recorded and, in the British Isles, they may arrive at any date throughout March. However, on average, the last week of March is the most favoured period for British puffins, with the exception of eastern Scotland, where, for some reason, the arrival may be a week or two earlier. In general, the more northerly the colony the later the arrival will be, with the Faeroes and Iceland expecting puffins in mid-April whereas Greenland birds are not expected until the middle of May. There would be little point in these more northerly birds arriving any earlier because the ground would still be frozen from the winter. North American birds arrive on average 2 weeks later.

In the introduction to this book, I gave the impression that there is a bond between the male and female which lasts from one year to the next. This suggests, of course, that there is a loyalty or permanent bond involved or why else would the pair re-unite when there are hundreds or thousands of other puffins to choose from. If they do not remain together throughout the autumn and winter, it is difficult to understand how they can recognise each other after 7 or 8 months of separation but the evidence of research shows that 85 per cent of puffins retain the same partner from one year to the next; therefore mate fidelity appears to be very strong. Ruth Ashcroft, in her research on Skomer Island, found that, if the pair did not re-unite, there was usually a very good reason, e.g. the death of one of the pair during the winter. Mate fidelity would be easier to understand if, in fact, the pair did remain in contact with each other throughout the winter. So one argument might be that the pair forms a relationship which lasts a lifetime and, if they remained loosely in contact with each other during the winter, the relationship could be a permanent bond or at least a habit. I would like to believe this explanation; it has an element of romance about it that befits the bird. However, mate fidelity cannot be assessed until the birds arrive at the nest burrow and so a more practical explanation comes to mind. The attraction, not only to the same colony but to the same nest burrow, is very strong. In one colony, it was found that 92 per cent of burrow-owners retained the same burrow year after year. Those birds that left their burrows were always forced to do so by circumstances such as a burrow collapsing. As a result of changing burrows, they were less successful in breeding. If a bird loses its mate for any reason the chances of it finding a new mate and breeding the following year in the same burrow are very high. In all probability, the previous breeding season would have been successful for the bird, so it seems logical for it to return to the location of its success. No doubt both birds of the pair will feel the same way, so they will be re-united at the nest site. Therefore, it may be a strong loyalty to the nest burrow which brings the pair together again year after year rather than loyalty to each other.

When the birds first arrive offshore, they drift around in small rafts of about twenty or thirty birds. They sometimes give the impression of being loosely in 'pairs'. It would be interesting to discover whether these actually were breeding pairs of birds because we could then assess whether it was nest- or mate-fidelity which drew the pair together again. Peter Corkhill in his research observed a pair of puffins that had been colour-ringed. When they arrived at the colony for what he believed to be the first time that season, they landed together. From this, he concluded that they were paired before they reached the nest site. My personal feeling, however, is that the attraction is to the nest site rather than to the mate and that it is as a result of this that the pair re-unite.

The comings and goings of the puffins during their first few weeks at the colony are difficult to predict or understand. After being present offshore for a day or two, the whole group may disappear again. A typical diary of events might include the following entries.

18 March Late afternoon, about twenty puffins in small groups outside the bay.

19 March A little earlier today, probably twice as many puffins outside bay. Came into bay just before dusk.

23 March Have not been any puffins in sight since 19 March. Where have they gone?

24 March Large numbers of puffins today, in excess of 200. Congregated offshore, then small groups moved into bay during evening.

25 March Large numbers again today, 200–300. Arrived mid-morning and came directly into bay. Dull afternoon – came onto land for first time. Probably about 300 birds on land out of the 1,500 that breed in this bay.

26 March No puffins.

27 March Few; far out to sea.

28 March No puffins.

30 March Hundreds of puffins in bay and on shore by mid-afternoon, probably about half the colony.

Over the next 3 or 4 weeks, the irregular cycle continues, birds being present and then absent. Numbers of pairs are also building up over that period of time.

In this very abbreviated diary, little indication is given of the weather conditions for each day. It may be supposed that it is the weather that affects the birds presence or absence at the colony. Indeed, very bad weather, rough sea and strong wind will keep puffins away from the colony initially. However, the weather conditions do not account for many situations. It is necessary for the puffins to travel a long distance to the feeding grounds at this time of year and it is important for them to feed well. The female needs to build up body condition ready for egg-laying and incubation, when meals will be few and far between. The bird's desire is divided between the need to feed well and the urge to be at the nest site. Its time must therefore be similarly divided.

If large numbers of birds arrive at the island together, presumably they all begin to feel the need to leave for the fishing grounds at the same time. There is a strong sense of the colony with the puffins now, so when a few birds prepare to leave, the others will join them. As a result, the nest cliffs may be deserted the next day. The rhythm of visits to and from the island have never been satisfactorily explained. It would appear that a basic 5-day rhythm within the bird is modified by the weather, the need to feed and social stimulation. This cycle of visits will end at egg-laying, when the need to incubate the egg constantly over-rides other instincts. I have referred to an island or a specific site as if it were one large colony, which in general is true. However, every colony appears to be divided into individual groups or sub-colonies and each bird reacts as part of its own smaller sub-colony. It is possible, therefore, to find that one part of the colony has a high percentage of birds present whilst the neighbouring sub-colony is deserted. The opposite may be true the following evening.

The first birds to arrive at the puffin colony are a pleasure to watch. They land during the evening, having congregated in the bay during the afternoon. As the light begins to fade, perhaps an hour before sunset, the birds fly over the cliff slopes two or three times before landing. The puffins stretch their wings and ruffle them into place as they flap. By their behaviour, it is easy to see that they are getting used to the solid environment of the land. They are very nervous, looking this way and that, taking fright at any sign of danger, real or imaginary. Preening seems to be overimportant, a nervous activity to help them settle down. They may potter about the colony for a few metres but, in general, the birds will have landed at the entrance to their old burrows. Surprisingly, soon after landing, they disappear down the burrows for a few minutes. Many birds just rest on the island for a while, content to simply stand outside their burrow entrances. As the light finally fades away so the puffins leave the island for the ocean. The next day there may be no puffins visible at all.

On their return, the number of puffins may have increased greatly and most of them settle into the colony. Many hundreds of them will have joined the advance party and these later birds will settle on the land without waiting in the bay. On the few occasions when puffins arrive at the colony late in the year, many thousands of birds may return together. In this situation, I have seen them land on the island on the first day. It seems as if numbers are needed to give each individual the confidence to land.

We have already seen that it is impossible to be certain where the pair of puffins first re-unite. Whether it is on the water or at the burrow, they waste little time in getting to know each other again. A bond is built up between the birds in two ways: through nest digging and through billing. Re-establishing the burrow is uppermost in both birds' minds and, by their mutual concern for this piece of property, the pair bond is strengthened. The birds arrive a little earlier each day to stand outside the burrow and demonstrate their ownership. Even on the first day of arrival, one or both of the pair may inspect the tunnel to ensure everything is in order. One bird may stand outside the burrow entrance looking deliberately down the tunnel and then back over its shoulder towards its partner, as a gesture of encouragement to its mate. In the days that follow, they do a little digging, both birds doing their share. One bird stands outside, as if on guard, while the other puffin is excavating. Difficult tasks and serious digging are accomplished by using the beak; the soil is loosened with powerful thrusts, grabs and twists. The loose soil is then scrabbled back using the webbed feet, which act as efficient shovels. Two channels a few

Overleaf: A muddy beak is an indication that the puffins are digging their burrows.

69

During billing, the pair face each other, wagging their beaks back and forth.

One pair billing often stimulates others to follow their example.

Whilst billing on the sea, the pair circle around in the water.

centimetres apart indicate where the individual feet have scored. The small ridge that is left in the centre becomes worn down through the season with the constant passage of puffin feet. While digging the burrow, the bird reverses out, kicking soil behind it with powerful thrusts. The soil showers out of the hole, forming a growing heap at the entrance. The unfortunate partner who is loyally waiting outside is often greeted with a hail of soil and stones. Shaking the soil from its feathers, it eagerly awaits the appearance of its mate. The puffins become quite dirty, with soil attached to beak and feet, and even the pure white chest becomes marred with soil. In the vast majority of cases, nest digging, at this stage, is quite unnecessary. The site would have been selected and prepared in previous years and, unless it had been damaged by weather or heavy-footed mammals, little would have changed. A tidy-up might be needed but excavation work is quite unnecessary. The digging appears to have two main purposes: it declares site ownership to other puffins and it builds up a strong attraction to the burrow and between the partners. In a few nest locations, such as the Farne Islands, new nest burrows do need to be dug more regularly due to the sandy nature of the soil.

As the puffin joins its mate, very excited billing takes place. Whether the puffin meets its mate after a bout of digging, when it arrives at the burrow or even on the water, billing is a very important part of courtship. The pair approach each other, one bird with its head low in a passive posture, whilst the other is more upright with its chin tucked in and chest puffed out. Their heads wag from side to side as they approach each other and, when they meet, their beaks are rapidly tapped together as their heads continue to wag back and forth. The rattling sound that they make by tapping their beaks together can be heard quite plainly. It appears to be very important to the puffins because it takes place at almost every available opportunity during the early stages of courtship and continues throughout the season to a lesser extent. A pair of birds billing on the water or on the land will attract the attention of the other puffins that are nearby. Determined not to miss out, they may begin to bill with their own partner. However, more often, they paddle or waddle in the direction of the courting couple and join in with them. On many occasions, I have seen four or even five birds circling around each other, billing with any of the group that will oblige – and even more puffins will be spectators. Possibly a kinship is developed between neighbours in this way, as well as an even greater sense of belonging to a colony, but this is purely speculation. Billing may last for a few moments or more than a minute and not only puffins seem to enjoy it; human spectators cannot help chuckling at this comical activity. Certainly, the act of billing is strongly associated with pair bonding. On a few occasions, it may lead to copulation but, to me, it does not usually seem to be

Courtship head flicking is used by the male to encourage the female.

associated with sexual activity. Associated with the desire to mate is another head-and-bill movement known as head flicking. Unlike billing, which may be instigated by either bird, head flicking is the male's attempt to persuade the female to copulate. For many hours, I have watched puffins on the water below the nest location and, throughout the whole of the build-up to copulation, it was only the male birds that performed head-flicking motions. Later in the season, and on the land, an activity similar to head flicking may be seen, although it occurs much less frequently and with less vigour. In this situation, it was impossible to determine the sex of the bird or to be positive about the purpose of the activity.

Copulation usually takes place on the sea, within a kilometre or so of the colony. The build-up to copulation begins with the male following the female wherever she goes. He constantly flicks his beak upwards so that, for a split second, it points to the sky. As the male becomes more persistent in his advances, the female moves away a little more quickly until it becomes almost a chase. At times I felt that the male was attempting to guide or drive the female away from the rest of the raft of puffins on the water but this did not always happen. Head flicking may become so pronounced that the male pursues the female for a few seconds with his beak pointing straight up. Another male may join him, also head flicking, and, although it is common to

As the male lunges towards the female, he turns his head sideways to show his beak to best advantage.

Wing flapping and preening always follows copulation.

With flapping wings, the male mounts the female and copulation takes place on the water.

see two birds following one female, the second male usually only remains with the pair for a few minutes. The pursuit may last for 20 minutes or more; occasionally the birds may bill with each other or even other puffins but, in general, the female keeps her distance, almost a metre away. It seems as if the female is attempting to escape the advances of the male but, if this were the case, why does she not fly away or dive beneath the surface of the water? Suddenly, it definitely becomes a chase and, as it gets faster and faster, weaving this way and that on the water, the male plunges after the female. He scampers over the water, using his wings as well as his feet to mount the female puffin. It is interesting to note that, when the male lunges after the female, he always has his head twisted to one side and does not look directly towards her. I concluded that, if the beak provided sexual stimulation to the female, as with head flicking, the sideways twist to the head would show the bill to its best advantage. If the female is receptive, the male stands on her back in a quite upright posture while, beneath the water, the female will twist her short tail to one side for copulation to take place. During mating, the male is constantly flapping his wings to maintain balance whilst the female's body is completely submerged, with only the head held high above the

75

water. At the precise moment of coition, the female may lift her rear end clear of the water. I only noticed this when I processed a sequence of photographs which I had taken, so it may not always be the case. The pair of birds circle around as the male stands on the female's back, flapping. Copulation may last from 30 seconds to a minute, or even longer. To conclude the mating, the female dives beneath the water, only to reappear a couple of metres away. The pair remain together for a while, violently flapping their wings as a prelude to a bout of preening. I am often intrigued by the predictability of some activities and wing flapping always takes place after copulation. It is probably either to settle ruffled feathers into place or a displacement activity.

One pair copulating definitely encourages other nearby males to attempt to mate with their partners. It is common for one pair to stimulate three or four other males to follow their example. Indeed, one male I saw become so excited that, every time a bird even flapped its wings nearby, it attempted to mount its harassed partner. A female does not co-operate with the male's advances on every occasion. I would estimate that only about one in ten attempts are accepted by the female. If the female is unreceptive, she will dive beneath the water to avoid the male as he lunges towards her. When she re-appears a metre or so away, wing flapping takes place and then the male generally continues to follow her about, flicking his head in encouragement.

Most puffin pairs seem to be very loyal to each other but sometimes flirtations do take place and some puffins may even attempt to mate with another bird's partner. One incident took place when a pair of birds were eagerly billing on the water. After only a couple of head flicking movements, the male attempted to mount the female but she was not receptive. She dived beneath the water to avoid him and, when the male continued to pursue her, she flew to the other side of the bay. Undeterred, the male turned to another nearby puffin and began to bill with that bird. As I watched him, I received the impression that it was an unpaired male; perhaps his mate had not returned to breed that year or had not yet arrived. On another occasion, a 'pair' were engaged in an enthusiastic bout of billing when a nearby male mounted the female and copulated with her. She accepted the new bird and was presumably fertilised by him; the previous partner did not seem to interfere. Which was the true mate? Would one male rear another male's chick? Plenty of questions sprung to mind but I could not get any answers as I watched the birds for the next 15 minutes before losing track of them amongst the hundreds of other puffins in the bay. It was only one odd situation and far from the usual method of mating. I also made a wooden model puffin and left it amongst the colony on the cliff top, where I found one bird attempting to mate with it.

76

When gathering nest material, the puffin may take large bundles or only a single stalk.

Mating on land takes place rather more often than I expected. It is sometimes a clumsy affair and probably not often successful. Nevertheless, after the customary head flicking, the female may accept the male by lowering her body, thereby allowing him to mount her. The flapping wings during mating, and even the predictable settling of feathers into place afterwards, are exactly the same as on the water. If the female is not receptive, she will remain upright or even fly out to sea. Head-flicking puffins at the colony are regularly seen and, when the female leaves for the water, the male will follow and continue his advances on the sea.

Once the burrow has been repossessed, the pair bond has been reestablished and the egg has been fertilised, a period of feeding and resting takes place before egg-laying begins. During this period of time, nest material may be gathered. The puffins' enthusiasm for collecting nest material varies greatly, not only from one colony to another but between individual birds within the same colony. It is doubtful whether a puffin actually needs a nest lining at all, except in situations where the birds are nesting in crevices between boulders. Some pairs lay their eggs on the bare soil with only a few dried stems left haphazardly in the burrow. Other puffins put a great deal of time and effort into collecting large quantities of material. I would hardly describe these large nests as tidy or carefully arranged; the material appears to be dumped on the floor in roughly the right place. The bird's body then forms a hollow as the puffin settles comfortably into place. Dead and dry vegetation is gathered with great determination, the birds tugging and heaving until their beaks are full. The bundle is then rushed down the burrow as if the delivery were of great urgency. However, not all puffins seem to understand why they have collected the material and many reappear at the burrow entrance with the bundle still in their beaks and, with a flick of their heads, allow the wind to blow it all away. Others may collect a few stems and then lose interest in them and drop them again.

At the end of the burrow, out of sight of direct light, the puffin lays its egg either on the bare soil or on the gathered nest material. Egg-laying begins during the first week of April in the earliest of the colonies but in the majority of British colonies it does not begin until the third week of April. Egg-laying continues for about a month, with a peak of eggs being laid in the first week of May. It is only possible to give a rough guide to the egg-laying dates because they vary each year and in each colony. In general, the more northerly colonies are correspondingly later; in Norway and Iceland, mid-May would be the earliest that eggs are laid. Greenland puffins do not begin to lay until early June. The peak of laying in Newfoundland occurs in the third week of May.

The puffin lays a single egg. It has been suggested that on rare occasions two eggs are laid but this is so uncommon and unlikely that it is best ignored. The egg is oval in shape and white in colour with, although very rarely, a few faint markings. The whiteness of the egg is lost during incubation as the surface becomes stained and soiled in the nest burrow. It is a very large egg compared with the size of the adult. It weighs 57–67 grams, which is about 14–15 per cent of the puffin's body weight. Measuring about 61 millimetres long and 42.5 millimetres across it is about the size of an average chicken's egg. The large size of the egg and long incubation period means that the chick is well developed when it hatches. All of the adults' attention is lavished on the single chick and, as a result, its chances of survival are very high.

It is interesting to compare the puffin with other species which produce perhaps seven eggs in a clutch, and are capable of two or even three broods in the year. These species have relatively short life spans and rely on the chance that two of the large number of chicks will survive to replace the parents within their short lifetimes. Such species are capable of rapid population expansion as well as rapid decline, in response to the changeable environments in which they live. The puffin's environment, on the other hand, is very stable and it is a long-lived bird. Therefore, for an adult to replace itself in its life-

Underground, the puffin sits patiently while incubating the egg.

time with one of its offspring, the best policy is to concentrate its efforts, each year, on raising only one chick that is strong and well developed before it has to fend for itself. Thus, as far as the puffin is concerned, we can describe the advantage of laying a single egg as being biologically efficient.

Incubation begins from the day the egg is first produced and extends for a period of 39–43 days. Both birds are involved, each taking a turn that may last from only an hour or two to more than a day. The incubating bird tucks the egg under its body and, on occasions, it seems to use a wing to hold it in place against the warm brood patch. Although it only lays a single egg, the puffin has two brood patches. These are areas of bare skin, situated on either flank, which have an enhanced supply of blood. They are only revealed when the feathers are parted. The bird may nibble a few feathers into place whilst sitting underground, or even peck at the odd grass stem that is irritating it.

However, in general, the parent spends most of the incubating period asleep with its head under its wing or staring down the tunnel in a trance-like state. The puffin does not incubate continually and will take a few moments off to potter outside, where it will flap the dust from out of its feathers and rest in the warmth of the sun. It may even fly out to sea for a while, returning within the hour to continue incubating. The egg is safe underground and does not chill quickly.

An egg that is lost or broken, by predation or some other misfortune, can be replaced. The replacement egg is usually laid about a fortnight after the loss of the first egg. It would seem that only eggs that are destroyed early in the incubation period can be replaced in this way. On average only 10 per cent of broken or lost eggs are replaced by the birds; the remaining unfortunate pairs will not rear a chick that year.

With all natural history subjects, it is difficult to know where to break into the cycle of the seasons. The puffin has a cycle of courtship that continues from one year to the next and I chose to join it at the beginning of the breeding season. We know that the puffin is likely to retain the same partner from one year to the next but, during their first visit to the colony as sub-adults, they have to form the initial

Puffins stand outside their burrows on a typical nest slope.

relationship. They are on average 3 years old when they first come ashore but a few 2-year-olds (rarely 1-year-olds) may arrive to inspect the colony. Some birds may be 6 years old before they breed and it is possible that these do not return to the breeding location until the year before breeding. These sub-adult birds do not arrive with the adults early in the season but drift into the colony from early May onwards, the main bulk arriving in late June and early July. It is as well that they wait for the adults to have settled into the breeding season because, when they arrive, they will be looking for a nest burrow.

Their courtship begins on the water. Probably they are stimulated to join with other puffins that are billing. The young courting birds form into rafts and continue the courtship activities that the adults no longer have time to indulge in (the adults have hungry beaks to fill and little time to waste). As the sub-adults shower onto the land during the summer evenings, they continue the quest for mate and burrow. Pair bonds are formed as burrow ownership is reinforced with regular bouts of billing. Billing is careless and is not as proficient as in the adults, but it is just as amusing to watch and appears to give as much pleasure to the birds, attracting many puffins from nearby. The young birds probably return to the colony for a few years, perfecting the nest burrow with a little digging and strengthening the pair bond. Puffins will first attempt to breed when 5 or 6 years old, although a small proportion may make their first attempt at the age of 3 or 4 years. The younger birds are not so likely to be successful. Many puffins wait until they reach 7 years or even older before they attempt to lay and hatch an egg.

With the increasing numbers of young birds arriving throughout the early summer, the colony swells in size. By mid-June and July, the bay is full of puffins resting on the water, the slopes are laden with birds parading outside their burrows and puffins are constantly flying in from the ocean with fish-laden beaks. The puffin colony is in full swing.

5 Chick Development

MANY years ago, R. M. Lockley asked the question 'Does the puffin expect a chick to hatch from out of the egg?' Does the bird expect this hard, apparently lifeless, stone-like object to break open and reveal a soft, warm, moving, living bird? It is a question that, in all probability, can never truly be answered but it leads us to marvel at the miracle of nature which we call instinct and which we take so much for granted. Whether or not the bird expects the egg to hatch does not concern the puffin because, when it happens, it certainly knows how to deal with the new life in the burrow. The chick is kept warm, fed and protected until it leaves the nest.

In the same way as the laying dates vary, so the hatching dates will also vary throughout the breeding range, as well as from season to season. As incubation lasts about 39–43 days, the majority of eggs will chip from mid-May onwards. It may be between 3 and 5 days after the first signs of hatching that the young chick finally emerges from the egg. During this period, the adults must become aware that there is life in the egg and that this new life will need a supply of fish to live. The first sign of the chick's arrival (from outside the burrow) is that the adults begin to land at the nest site with fish-laden beaks. I always find the arrival of the first fish-carrying puffins an exciting moment, an indication of successful hatching. This may begin in early May but, in general, hatching does not take place until the second half of May and throughout June. Around the British coast, some chicks may still be hatching in July and, of course, further north this is even more common. In Greenland, for example, many birds will not be laying until early June and, therefore, their offspring will not hatch until mid-July.

The male and female puffins share the responsibility of rearing the chick. Both birds bring a supply of fish to the nest and either male or female will brood the young bird. Occasionally one of a pair is killed by a predator. If this happens then the remaining adult can easily raise the chick alone. There are many records of this happening and, when

puffins were regularly trapped at the nest, the ability of a single adult to raise the chick was essential for its survival.

When the chick emerges from the egg, it gives the impression of being completely helpless. It is black in colour, and wet, and looks most unappealing. As the down quickly dries, the chick's true characters appear. Within only half an hour it can be seen that the young bird is completely covered in a wonderfully fluffy, soft down and is perfectly capable of standing quite firmly on its large feet. The colour of the down on the majority of the chick is glossy black but its belly and chest merge in a pale cream colour. The weight of this little bundle of fluff is about 40–45 grams and it looks most appealing, resembling a ball supported on grey legs and extra large webbed feet. Little black eyes twinkle in the small amount of light that filters down the burrow and its beak, unlike that of its parents, is of a more conventional bird shape, although rather large and stocky compared with the size of the chick. The beak is grey in colour and has a creamy yellow gape showing clearly at the base. The egg tooth, which shows as a pale tip to the beak, remains with it for several weeks before falling off.

At this early stage, the chick is constantly attended by its parents and, for the majority of the time, it is brooded by one or other of the adults. Not until 2 or 3 days have passed is the chick left on its own for

any length of time. Whilst it is assisted by its parents' body warmth, the chick's ability to convert food into body weight is amazing. The adults will bring beakfuls of fish to the youngsters only two or three times a day and the daily intake of the chick averages about 20 grams at this stage. However, the small chick is able to convert this food very efficiently and can gain as much as 10 grams of body weight per day. The fish are supplied whole to the youngster and are in no way pre-digested, as is the case with many other birds. Once the parents stop brooding the chick, the food conversion rate becomes less efficient but, with both parents now fishing for their offspring, the supply of fish is increased. As a result, the chick growth rate is maintained at 10 or 11 grams per day until it is about 3 weeks old.

About 70–75 per cent of the chick's day consists of sleeping or resting at the end of the burrow. When watching the youngsters underground, it is fascinating to see how active they are, even from the very early stages. The chick seems to have a fascination for every item of nest material which is not in precisely the correct place. It will carry the offending grass stem a little way up the burrow, turn around and put it down again exactly where it was before. Satisfied with this pointless exercise, it may rest for a few moments before repeating the operation with another, or even the same, stem. Stone-picking is an-other activity that seems pointless; the chick picks up a stone which it

At 6 days old, the chick is exercising its wings.

84

carries about for a few moments before losing interest in it and dropping it back onto the floor of the burrow. Watching this behaviour from only about half a metre away, it is difficult not to speculate on the purpose of these activities. It is possible that sitting in the gloomy atmosphere of the nest burrow prompts the youngster to find some occupation to fill its day. On the occasions when a chick picks up a stone, it is probably searching for fish that have been left behind after its last meal. Once the stone is found to be inedible, it is simply dropped. Watching the hatchling struggling to take hold of a little root growing through the roof of the burrow is most entertaining. It also illustrates that the chick is rather clumsy and needs a great deal of practice before being as proficient as its parents. Pulling roots, carrying nest material and picking up stones all amount to excellent practice and, whether through boredom or hunger, the chick soon learns.

Even during the first few days of life, exercise appears to take up a large proportion of the chick's active periods. As one might expect, wing exercise is common, with violent wing flapping causing a mini dust storm in the burrow. At times, individual wings are stretched to their maximum, first one wing then the other, before being settled into place again with a quick shake of the body. More interesting to observe was some rather strange behaviour that, at first, was hard to

explain. The young chick would face the end of the burrow, with its chest against the solid wall of soil, and then push and strain with its legs and webbed feet, as if trying to force a way through. Again these efforts seemed pointless because the chick only scrabbled the soil backwards and covered the nest material with debris. However, so persistent was the young bird that it quickly became apparent that these were leg and foot exercises. On reflection, the need to be able to use these muscles to paddle in the water is far greater than the need for strong flight muscles, as will be seen when we discuss the young leaving the nest.

At about a week old, the character of the young bird seems to change. In appearance, it is only a larger version of the recently-hatched chick. The bird becomes much less active and a greater proportion of the chick's time is spent resting or sleeping. Often the youngster's head will slowly lower until its beak rests on the ground and its eyes are closed. It will also sleep with head doubled back over its shoulder and beak tucked under its wing. Rest periods may be a little shorter but periods of activity are considerably shorter. Legs and wings may only be exercised for a moment or two before the bird settles down again to rest. The whole attitude of the chick is more lethargic and sluggish as the young bird becomes fat and heavy and appears to have difficulty even in walking. Growth rate continues at

This fat youngster spends hours simply resting in the darkness.

about 10 or 11 grams each day until the chick is about 3 weeks old. During the fourth week, the speed of growth will slowly decline to only 8 grams a day. The fish supply brought in by both parents increases steadily for the first 4 weeks in the nest, until probably ten loads of fish are dropped in front of the youngster each day. Clearly, the size of each beakful of fish varies considerably, ranging from below 2 grams to over 18 grams. It is amazing to see a puffin deposit twenty-two fish in front of a chick from only one beakful; alternatively it is sometimes a little comical to watch a bird carry only three fish back to its nest burrow. However, the average weight of each load of fish would be about 8 grams and an average total weight of fish provided for a month-old chick is 75–100 grams each day.

From dawn until about 8 a.m., the adult birds concentrate their efforts on feeding the youngsters underground in the burrows. The sky is busy with puffins flying from, or returning to, the nest site, bringing in loads of fish carried sideways across their beaks. It has been suggested that the fish are always stacked alternately, head to tail, along the length of the adult's beak. This is not the case and observation will show that they are held completely at random. However, on occasions, the overall effect certainly gives the impression of some very precise arranging of the fish. It is during this morning period that the young birds receive probably 60–70 per cent of their daily intake of fish. During the heat of the day, the supply of fish is greatly reduced and comparatively few birds are seen standing near their burrows or bringing fish to the cliff tops. In the late afternoon, the numbers begin to build up and once again, throughout the evening, the chicks are provided with as much food as they can eat.

Underground, the chick sees nothing of the activity that is taking place just above its head. Its world is made up of the darkness of the chamber, the light filtering down the tunnel and a great variety of sounds. Having spent many hours in the darkness watching chicks underground, it was interesting to try and assess the activity of the outside world by sounds alone. The fast whirring wing beats of the adult birds were easy to identify and it was possible to distinguish between a bird landing, taking off or just flying past. Even the footsteps of puffins could be distinguished and, of course, the low gentle growling calls could be heard all around. Even from quite an early stage, the chick seemed able to differentiate between the sounds and its period of activity would coincide with puffin sounds outside.

Overleaf: A bird prepares to land with fish at the burrow entrance. Adults (inset) fly back and forth, bringing a constant supply of fish.

Wing beats that stopped nearby might prompt the chick to potter a few steps along the tunnel, whilst a sudden flurry of wings taking off would send it rushing back down to the safety of the nest. The chick would never have seen a greater blackbacked gull swooping at a party of puffins on the cliff top but it could somehow sense the danger from the urgent sound of the adult wings. A puffin chick will also respond

in alarm to the call of a nearby gull, its inbred fear showing from even the earliest age. If a puffin chick is removed from the burrow and allowed to stand on the soil nearby, its immediate reaction is to dash for the nearest dark hole it can find. If a burrow is not available, then the darkest area possible will suffice; it may even be under a jacket lying on the ground. The chick's fear of the daylight and love of dark corners has a great survival value when retreating from predators and remains with it until the day it leaves the nest. An unfamiliar shadow cast at the entrance of the burrow will cause the chick to back away in fright but, somehow, it can identify a puffin in the burrow, even when it is not its parent. On one occasion, a puffin began to enter the entrance of the burrow and the chick got to its feet and pottered up the tunnel towards the incoming bird. The chick seemed aware that it was not one of its parents because it was not full of its usual enthusiasm and excitement. Nevertheless, the chick disappeared from sight around a bend in the burrow towards the entrance. The next moment it came scampering back, almost falling over itself in distress. The incoming puffin was a sub-adult bird searching for an empty nest hole ready for the next year's breeding season. The chick had become a little too inquisitive and had received a nasty peck on the neck. Within moments, it had got over its experience, realising that it was in no real danger.

From watching the behaviour of puffin chicks, there can be no doubt that they have some method of knowing when the adult bird is about to arrive with food. Even before the parent bird has landed (sometimes 3 or 4 minutes before), the youngster becomes very excited and active. It will suddenly jump to its feet and make its way up the tunnel a short distance, stopping only to preen a little and flutter any dust from out of its feathers. Facing the burrow entrance, it will wait, calling at regular intervals with a soft *peeping* sound, usually a double call *peep-peep*, a gentle rather than a penetrating sound. A rapid whirring of wings and a parent enters the tunnel, blocking out the light as it arrives. How the chick knows it is coming is a mystery, neither calls nor wing beats of a bird landing nearby seemed to be the answer. Is it possible that the chick can identify the sound of its parent's wings from amongst so many others as it flies past in preparation for landing?

The adult bird can be heard coming down the burrow as it softly growls a call to the youngster. When it approaches nearer, each footstep can plainly be heard and the chick rushes to greet its parent with great enthusiasm. Although the young bird may have gone over half a metre up the burrow to meet the adult, it is not fed there and the chick reverses back as the parent comes in. At the nest site, it was interesting to see the chick grabbing at the parent's beak. At first I presumed it was aiming for the fish that the parent was carrying but

A large number of sandeels are stacked neatly across the beak.

In the depths of the
burrow, a supply of
sand-eels are fed to the
youngster.

The adult puffin turns
around and patters its
way to the burrow
entrance.

the youngster seemed fairly insistent on this behaviour until the fish were dropped onto the floor of the burrow. Confused by this behaviour, I watched fish being given to the chick on several occasions and, each time, a similar activity took place. A photograph captured the chick with its head turned sideways holding the beak of the adult bird. Surely if the youngster was aiming for the fish it would not turn its head sideways? This may not have been a typical youngster but I felt it was an interesting observation. The parent sheds either the whole or part of the load of fish in front of the chick and the chick then leaves the adult for the more interesting prospect of the silvery fish on the floor. If the adult has shed its whole load, it will wait for a moment or two, watching its offspring begin the feast. An adult that has retained some of its fish in its beak will back off and wait until the chick has finished and calls for more with plaintive cheeps; it will then move forward to feed it again. On one occasion, an adult stole a fish from under the nose of the youngster and swallowed it, as if in payment for the effort of catching the fish.

The first few fish of the puffin's meal are swallowed quickly and greedily, one after the other. They are grabbed from the floor and gulped down, head or tail first, or even attempted sideways, in the bird's eagerness to devour them. As the youngster's crop fills, so the effort of swallowing them increases, until the final fish may be eaten only with a great struggle. As the last fish is swallowed, with straining, choking movements, the young bird's neck visibly bulges beneath the fluffy down. With its crop stuffed to capacity, the bird will settle to rest. It may sleep with its eyes closed and beak lowered to the floor for over an hour. Should the other adult arrive during that rest period, however, the chick will once again leap into action as if it were starved. This time it may not manage all the fish and a few will be left for after the rest period.

On waking, the chick will stretch its limbs, straining its legs backwards and flapping with the undeveloped wings, sending up yet another dust cloud. The smell of the burrow is quite strong, a sickly fishy smell of ammonia that makes your eyes sting. The puffin potters along the burrow to either a bend in the tunnel or a side passage where it will then turn and forcibly defaecate away from the nest area. This habit keeps the nest area clean and a small midden of black and white excrement builds up in one place.

At 4 weeks old, the chick is still underground and, surprisingly, it appears to be covered in the soft down even at this late stage. However, beneath the layer of down, the feathers are almost completely developed. As the chick scuffs the rough soil walls of the burrow, it is protected from abrasion by the fluffy down. The chick is now approaching its maximum weight of around 320 grams very rapidly. The fish supply has increased until this stage and the chick will probably be consuming about 80 grams of fish a day; this is about 25 per cent of its own body weight. Two changes take place at this stage and it is difficult to know which change is the cause and which the effect. The bird stops putting on weight and it also becomes active once again. At about the same time, the adults begin to reduce the supply of fish to around 55–65 grams. Possibly it is because of the reduction in fish supplies that the bird becomes hungry and therefore active again. As a result of this newfound activity, the bird may use up its energy and stop putting on weight. Or it may be that the reduction in food prevents the puffin gaining weight and, as a result, it becomes capable of great activity again. Whatever the reason, the young puffin now seems determined to become fit rather than fat.

A much higher proportion of its time is spent pottering back and forth along the burrow. Some of the bird's wanderings may take it into side passages that it has not investigated until this late stage. It is possible that it will meet with another puffin chick underground but strangely, company is not appreciated and the two young birds will fight quite violently beneath the ground. It is said that, if two puffin chicks are put into a cardboard box, they will attack each other, even in that strange environment. There are a few claims that puffins will on rare occasions lay two eggs and I wonder, if both were to hatch, whether the chicks would fight. It is during the last week in the nest that the chick may view the outside world for the first time. The attraction of the daylight must grow stronger and stronger until it cannot resist a fearful peak out of the burrow. It will strain its neck to see, peering in all directions and turning its head to get a better view. A few chicks may even come right out of the burrow and stand in the entrance for a while with the adult birds. Although only the occasional youngster behaves in this way, it is possible to see one at the entrance to its burrow, exercising its wings with violent flapping movements. The appearance of a young bird seems to concern the adults, who behave in an agitated manner. On one or two occasions, I have observed immature birds, attracted by the chicks' flapping, who have walked over and attempted to bill with them. It has always been in the evening when large numbers of adult birds are present at the colony that the chicks venture out. At any sign of danger, real or imaginary, the little puffin dives for its life into the darkness of the burrow.

Although the puffin may move about the burrow, if it is frightened it will always scuttle back to the secure feeling of the nest site. It is also only fed at the nest location and it appears to be the sight or sounds of a bird in the correct place that stimulates the adult puffin to drop the supply of fish. For example, if two chicks were to swap nests, the adult will continue to feed the same nest and the wrong chick. Various experiments were tried where chicks of different ages were exchanged and the adult still did not appear to notice, even though the chick had suddenly quadrupled in size or had reverted back to a freshly-hatched bird. Also the adult continued to feed them as if the exchange had not been made. So the large birds only received a meagre portion each day whilst the little chick had an ample supply. It would seem, therefore, that the adult puffin responds more to the nest site than to its offspring, which may reflect a similar attitude to nest- and mate-fidelity. I have even known a puffin to enter a burrow and leave its fish on the bare floor after the young bird had left the nest. However, on other occasions, I have seen adult birds coming out of a burrow with fish still in their beaks, presumably because they could not find a young bird beneath the ground to feed.

Throughout its development, the puffin has exercised its leg muscles by digging in the burrow. Kicking and scrabbling soil from one side of the burrow to the other takes up quite a lot of the chick's time and effort, especially in the early stage. Once again, in its final week, this activity takes on a renewed importance. However, this time, it is not just a little digging for the sake of exercise; the bird now begins to excavate in earnest. I have seen the bird really attack the back wall of the burrow with powerful pecks of its beak, struggling to remove stones and roots with incredible determination. The soil is forced back with powerful leg thrusts and the webbed feet make very efficient shovels. The slight depression which contained a few bits of nest material, and which the chick regarded as its nest, now becomes covered in the rubble of the excavation and the youngster is no longer concerned about the nest. An adult bird that arrives to feed the energetic chick may have to negotiate a pile of soil and then have the greatest difficulty turning around to leave the nest. Adult puffins always turn around when underground so as to leave the nest forwards. To come out of a burrow backwards would clearly be a dangerous thing to do with many predators lying in ambush.

The fledgling period is variable with the puffin. It may range from 34–50 days, although 38–44 days would be more common. The variation is due mainly to the supply of fish in the area and, if food is in short supply, then a whole colony may take longer to fledge their youngsters. Young puffins underground may need to go without food on occasions. They are quite capable of doing this and draw on their reserves of body fat. As a result they are able to lose weight as fast as they are able to gain it. Fledging seems largely controlled by the chick's body weight because, in most situations, the youngsters achieve about 70–80 per cent of adult weight before leaving the burrow. In certain extreme situations, a bird may be reared in the nest by the adult for 60–80 days before it is large enough to leave for the sea. The chick is in no way starved out of the nest by its parents. For many years, this was thought to be the case but the fact that an adult will

continue to feed a chick until it is, maybe, 80 days old must illustrate otherwise. On several occasions, puffins have been observed bringing a supply of fish to the nest the day after the youngster has left – evidence again that the chick is not starved out. The food supply is definitely reduced during the last 10 days, as we have seen, and the puffin will actually lose weight during the final 3 or 4 days underground. The peak weight of around 320 grams is reduced to a fledging weight of 290–295 grams. Although fledging weights will be comparatively higher in the more northerly subspecies, a loss of about 10 per cent is usual.

It is not until the last few days in the nest that the puffin moults the soft down which kept it warm as a freshly-hatched chick. For a week or so, the light, silvery grey, crescent-shaped area behind the eye becomes increasingly obvious. Suddenly the down moults in only 3 or 4 days, filling the burrow with fluff that mixes with the soil. As the down is shed, the chick can be seen to be fully feathered with a glossy black plumage. The crescent-shaped, silver-grey cheeks stand out clearly because the area between the eye and the bill is dark grey. The underside of the bird is completely white. The legs, feet and beak are a light grey colour.

Many young puffins will leave their burrows during July; further north they will be correspondingly later. By the second week of

When the down is shed, the juvenile's glossy plumage is revealed.

At nightfall, a fledgling walks out of the burrow and makes its way to the sea.

August, only a few British puffins will be feeding young underground. A few late stragglers may continue carrying fish ashore into September but this is exceptional and is probably the result of a late replacement egg. On a dark night, as the gulls begin to settle, the puffin chick appears at the burrow entrance. On this occasion, it does not hesitate for long but half scampers, half flutters in a fairly direct line towards the sea. Dozens of puffins may be seen scurrying towards the cliff edge on a good night, the odd wisp of down visible on their new shiny plumage. How the young puffin knows which direction to take we cannot be sure but presumably it follows the sound of the waves or keeps heading downhill. Apparently unaware of the cliff edge, it tumbles over and flutters down towards the ocean. The juvenile puffin is totally on its own and will not have any contact with its parents again. It is in an environment of water, constantly moving, cold and exposed. What a complete change to the warm, solid security of the nest burrow that it left only a few minutes ago. Instincts within the puffin drive it in the direction of the open ocean and, by dawn, it will be well out to sea. The urge to leave the nest during the first half of the night enables the young bird to avoid the predatory gulls under cover of darkness. If a chick attempts to leave the colony during even the twilight hours its chances of escaping the marauding gulls are slim. Gulls are well aware of the potential meals that lie underground and

97

regularly inspect the burrows for any chicks that have foolishly ventured too near the entrance. Success from hatching to fledging is
nevertheless high, with about 95 per cent of the chicks flying to the
sea. The chicks of first-year breeding birds may not be quite as successful due to their inexperience.

On route to the ocean,
the fledgling may try its
wings for a few
moments.

Once the chick is on the water, it is comparatively safe from avian
predators because, as soon as it comes in contact with the sea, it is
capable of diving. It has been suggested that the first reaction of the
young puffin is to dive beneath the water for about 20 seconds.
Having surfaced it will then almost immediately dive again, time after
time until away from the land. R. Lockley suggested 'an inborn desire
to hide . . . looking for a refuge'. This may be the case but I have found
it impossible to observe puffin chicks on the water in a completely
natural way. If a torch is used to observe the chicks on a dark night,
the birds may dive out of fear of the torchlight. If the youngsters are
captured and released in the daylight they are able to see the observer
and so, once again, they may dive out of fear. The young birds are
certainly capable of diving deeply and remain under water for a long
time. However, I would guess that the chicks paddle away from the
colony, using their webbed feet, rather than swimming beneath the

water for a long distance. It is possible for a bird to be at least 3 kilometres out before daylight.

The young puffins do not appear to be attracted towards each other or, indeed, to the adults. They continue paddling out to sea and will not return to land for 2 or even 3 years. In the meantime they live a lonely existence.

6 Mortality and Kleptoparasitism

THE puffin preys upon fish for its existence and, in its turn, the puffin is preyed upon by many other species of animal. Avian predators in particular pursue the puffin; land mammals can also be a problem and, at certain colonies, even human beings take their toll. The bird is never entirely safe from predators. When on the water, it is also at risk from pollution; even adverse weather conditions threaten the birds. It would be fair to say that, without the losses that I have outlined above, the puffin population would be held in check only by its food supply. Many instances of natural predation occur and, although the sight of a gull eating a puffin chick may seem rather sad, few of us are affected by a puffin chick swallowing a fish. Predators are a necessary part of a puffin's life, or death, as are the instances of natural loss. Pollution of the sea, by oil or chemicals, is a problem which the puffin has no method of combating and, as a result, it may develop into a long-term problem that only we can correct. Man's detrimental effect on the puffin's environment may be more subtle than oil pollution; it may just tip the balance between prey and predator, and another colony of puffins can be lost.

The puffin has a potentially long life span, with only 5 per cent of the adult population dying each year, in spite of the attention of so many predators. The 95 per cent survival rate indicates an average life span of about 25 years and many birds are on record as having achieved that age and are still going strong. The oldest puffins that have been ringed are now 30 years old and future years will reveal more information about life span. It is frightening to study the survival rate and population dynamics calculated by Dr Mike Harris. If, by affecting the environment, we reduce the adult survival rate by only 1 per cent, the puffin's life expectancy is reduced from 25 years to only 21 years – only sixteen breeding seasons instead of twenty. This means four (or 20 per cent) less breeding seasons to raise youngsters as replacements, and likewise for the youngsters, so slowly the population melts away.

We know the puffin lays only one egg but the chances of the egg hatching successfully is high. The success to fledging is also very high and a good proportion of the fledglings will return to breed at the colony. To maintain population numbers, it is important that the adults successfully replace themselves during their lifetime. Figures indicating breeding success and survival to fledging vary widely from colony to colony, and even from year to year. I will select what may be considered average results and, for the sake of simplicity, omit extreme situations that may be the result of human disturbance caused by research. Puffins do not necessarily attempt to breed every year and, of the adult birds associated with a colony, only 80 per cent will attempt to breed in any single year. These birds, having laid an egg, will have a 60–85 per cent chance of hatching a chick, an average of 75 per cent. A very high proportion of the chicks will fledge, with only 5 per cent being lost; this means that approximately 72 per cent of the breeding pairs will rear a chick to fledge. Many youngsters will die during the first 6 months at sea. The remaining years, before breeding age is achieved, will also take their toll. About 20–40 per cent of the youngsters which fledge will attain full breeding status at 5 years of age. A pair of puffins will therefore live for an average of 25 years and these will include twenty breeding seasons. They will only attempt to breed on 80 per cent of these occasions, i.e. sixteen times. Assuming that they continue to be an average pair of puffins, they will raise about eleven or twelve chicks in their lifetime. If 30 per cent of these fledglings survive to breed, then the 2 adults will be replaced by about 3.5 of their offspring. This implies an increase of 75 per cent over 25 years, or 3 per cent each year, which is probably fairly near the truth. However, beware of these figures. We have seen that a 1 per cent loss in the adult survival rate removes four breeding seasons. In the same way, small changes in fledging success or juvenile survival have dramatic long-term effects.

It seems unlikely that many birds die from old age, the potential life span will be cut short by some form of predation or environmental condition. No doubt, on some occasions, the age of the bird is a contributing factor to its death, e.g. an aged bird may be slower to react to a predator. However, once the puffin has survived the first critical winter, the percentage mortality remains fairly constant. The effect of a long breeding season does not affect the puffin's chances of survival because birds which have bred seem just as likely to survive as those which did not rear a chick that year.

Because the puffin is such an attractive food source, the nest colonies encourage a high population of predators. The puffin is most vulnerable when it is on the land. However, it will attempt to defend itself, pecking violently with its beak and using its needle-sharp claws to scratch the predator. A puffin that is captured for ringing is not a passive bird (as many other birds are) and will constantly fight and wriggle. Its reaction is to struggle, trying to escape to the sea and the safety of the waves.

Puffins are not successful when ground predators are in evidence. Mammals are capable of causing havoc with the colony and, as a result, the majority of large and thriving colonies are on islands where foxes, rats, stoats, etc. are unable to invade. Not only are the adult birds taken by mammals, the chicks and eggs are also slaughtered. It is not difficult to imagine the damage to a colony that Arctic or red foxes could do, catching both the adults at the cliff top and the chick in the burrow. Otters, mink, stoats and weasels can easily take adults, chicks and eggs from burrows. Wild cats as well as domestic cats will also take puffins. On one occasion I observed a feral cat stalking a puffin. This so irritated me that I threw a clod of earth in its direction which frightened off the puffin. I doubt if I would have reacted in this way if the cat had been a wild cat in the Scottish highlands; how fickle we human beings are! Rats have caused the downfall of many colonies over the years. If introduced accidentally by Man, a rat population will rapidly expand until the puffins desert the island for a more suitable breeding site. Rats certainly take the eggs and even chicks from the burrows but I doubt whether they kill the adult birds. However, the adults would possibly desert anyway after several years of failing to raise a chick successfully.

I had often wondered whether seals took puffins from the water. It seemed fairly probable because, on many occasions, I have seen seals stalking slowly towards a raft of puffins and the puffins looking down into the depths and appearing most agitated. Recently, an excited lady described an incident that had taken place only moments before. Apparently she had been watching the puffins on the water beneath the cliff. In the bay, about 30 metres away, she had seen a dark shape beneath the water which was thought to be a seal; the lady was familiar with the island and knew the seals' habits. The seal was lost from view and so the lady returned her attention, and binoculars, to the puffins. Suddenly the shape reappeared beneath the puffins, exploding out of the water with its mouth wide open. It had emerged directly beneath one puffin which, for a second, was held aloft in its jaws. The seal then dived too deeply to be followed, taking the puffin into the depths. The lady had no idea of my special interest in puffins when she shared her experience with me and, on questioning her further, I found out about a strange reaction from the other puffins in the area. Most of the birds, which numbered about fifty, flew off as one might expect. scampering along the water in fright. About eight birds were very close to the attacked puffin and the first reaction of these birds was to dive. I hardly need say that they reappeared very quickly, leaping out of the water, to fly off with the rest. It is interesting to see

Peering into the water, a puffin checks that there are no predators beneath the surface.

that, in extreme panic, the puffin will dive for safety, even if it is the wrong thing to do, as on this occasion.

In general, once the bird is on the water, it is fairly safe from predators. Certainly the puffins are constantly looking beneath the surface but this need not necessarily be fear of predation. It seems possible that large fish might enjoy a puffin meal but the only evidence of this on record is of an angler fish which was found to have a puffin in its stomach. An angler fish is a slow, bottom-feeding fish of deep water. One would expect a fast, large surface-feeder, such as a shark, to be more likely to attack a puffin. One-legged puffins are not uncommon at the colony. Perhaps a fish can answer the question 'Where did the other leg go?'

Attacks from the air are a far greater threat to the puffin, with the greater blackbacked gull taking more adult birds than all other natural predators put together. These birds are specialist feeders. By this, I do not mean that they take only one type of food but rather that individual birds or, quite often, pairs, develop a technique for making use of a specific food source. The food source may be offal from fishing boats or Man's waste at rubbish tips. It could be that a pair becomes adept at catching baby rabbits or Manx shearwaters which have not

hidden themselves underground by daybreak. Greater blackbacked gulls breed on many islands where there are puffin colonies and find the puffin a good source of food. Once a food source becomes available, some gulls will concentrate their efforts to the exclusion of most other foods. If a greater blackbacked gull is feeding its young on puffins for example, it will probably ignore a young rabbit nearby. The popularity of puffin-hunting varies greatly from one colony to another. In some locations, a high proportion of these gulls pursue the puffins; in others the proportion is much lower. Each gull may take one or two birds a day whilst the puffins are at the colony, even more when the gull chicks are growing fast. Only a few pairs specialising in this form of predation may therefore take hundreds of puffins throughout the season. Surprisingly, colonies that suffer heavy predation from the greater blackbacked gulls do not seem to be adversely affected. In fact, many of them are expanding in numbers.

Fortunately for the puffins, the greater blackbacked gull has not yet mastered the technique of capturing the birds on the ground. The method which it adopts is to drift lazily above the cliff top on the up-current of air, watching the puffins arriving at the colony. One can even see the gull's head turning, watching the approaching birds as it waits for a suitable puffin to fly into its hunting territory. It does not waste its energy attacking a large party of puffins but waits for a lone

A lesser blackbacked gull stalks a puffin but with little chance of success.

The remains of a puffin are left beside a gull's nest.

individual. Slipping to the rear of the bird, it pursues the puffin from behind and slightly above, taking advantage of the puffin's blind spot. If the puffin observes it soon enough, it will probably evade the gull, and a great many are able to escape. A puffin that is caught in mid-air has little chance and I have seen the powerful beak of a greater black-back gull clamp into a puffin on many occasions. Held by its wing, body or head, it is often shaken senseless in mid-air. It is then some-times beaten to death on a rock once the gull has landed. The meal is not yet the gull's because a few greater blackbacked gulls steal puffins from their own kind. The carcase is usually pecked clean, starting from the belly and breast and the skin is left turned inside out, like a discarded glove.

Lesser blackbacked gulls and herring gulls probably take extremely few puffins, although we will see how they pressurise the puffin colony with their piratical activities. They also directly prey on the colony by killing the young and stealing eggs. These two species can be watched parading through the colony, strutting from one burrow to the next. Cocking their heads, they peer down the burrow in the hopes that an egg may have rolled near the entrance, or a chick may have ventured too far up the tunnel. It is only the careless or weak puffins that are caught out by these tactics, although the chicks to tend to move towards the entrance to defaecate. The herring gulls and lesser blackbacked gulls will attempt to capture and kill the fledgling puffin chicks. As the youngsters leave the burrows, the gulls will attack. This is plainly the reason why puffins leave the nest after nightfall, when the gulls have settled, and so comparatively few fled-glings are lost this way.

A few other avian predators also prey on the puffin colony. In some colonies ravens will take many adults in the same way as do the larger gulls. I have seen a pair of jackdaws working as a team to steal puffin eggs. Whilst one jackdaw pestered and harried the adult puffin, the other stole the egg. These jackdaws were even prepared to go into the burrow (they themselves, of course, are burrow-nesting birds). Great skuas take puffins in a similar way to the greater blackbacked gulls but, in general, numbers of puffins killed in this way are few. No doubt any member of the crow family would steal the puffins' eggs and many birds of prey, including buzzards, eagles and owls, will take adults given the opportunity. Peregrine and gyr falcons breeding in the locations of puffin colonies regularly prey on them.

On 19 June, I watched a peregrine falcon drifting high along the cliffs of a puffin island. It slipped across the wind in a casual effortless glide and gave me no impression that it was hunting. The puffins that were all around me on the cliff top were not so easily fooled because the ones that were several metres from the cliff edge began to make their way to the sheer drop. They hurriedly waddled in short bursts, stopping to cock their heads to observe the falcon. Once at the cliff edge, they seemed less concerned. The peregrine was still very high but without a wing beat it began to gain speed and suddenly I knew the falcon was hunting. As the puffins left the cliff top in unison, the peregrine drew back its wings and dropped like a bullet. The puffins had assessed the situation to perfection and would reach the protection of the water without any losses. A few metres to my right a puffin walked straight out of its burrow and, finding itself alone, it looked about to see what had panicked the other birds. If only it had turned and walked back down the burrow, it would have lived. The bird scrambled for the cliff top to fly at full speed for the ocean. The peregrine must have realised it was going to be successful as it altered its course only a little. The panic flight of the puffin seemed painfully slow as the peregrine rapidly overtook it. Just a few metres from me, the peregrine hit the puffin. The jolting strike, the flurry of feathers and the dull thud were plain to my eyes and ears. The falcon smashed the bird to the ground and, with a few vicious pecks to the head, killed the puffin within seconds. Struggling with the weight of the puffin, the peregrine attempted to lift the bird. With heavy and laboured wing beats, the peregrine carried its prey away, out of sight around the headland. Perhaps I should have felt sad at the death of a puffin but the speed, precision and drama of the peregrine left me sitting on the cliff top reliving the moment with excitement. After 15 minutes I left and, by then, the puffins had returned, as many as before, quite unconcerned.

Strangely, it can be activity underground that causes the loss of many eggs. On islands where Manx shearwaters are breeding alongside the puffins, there is a certain amount of competition for the burrows. Shearwaters commonly go down puffin burrows as they visit the island after dark and, no doubt, the puffin would attempt to defend its burrow. When the shearwaters are digging in their burrows, it is not unusual to discover that they have dug into another burrow, possibly a puffin's. It has been estimated that 5–10 per cent of puffins' eggs are lost each year as the result of this kind of disturbance. Disturbance caused, for example, by other puffins, Manx shearwaters and eggs stolen by jackdaws may, in some colonies, account for a total loss of 25 per cent of puffin eggs. If the egg is lost early during the incubation period, another may be laid and, indeed, about 12 per cent of these lost eggs are replaced.

In many areas of the world, sea-bird 'wrecks' occur. Many thousands of birds are found dead or dying along the tide lines and scattered on the beaches. This is quite a separate problem from that of oil pollution, where birds may also be found in large numbers on the coast. All species of sea birds are affected, particularly members of the auk family, and the puffin suffers along with the rest of the auks. The majority of wrecks are associated with very stormy conditions at sea and periods of gale-force winds. It is often following these conditions that the birds are washed onto the beaches.

A massive wreck occurred in February 1983, when huge numbers of sea birds were recovered in the north and east of Scotland and England. In the area of highest fatality, up to 70 birds per kilometre were retrieved from the beaches. The total number recovered from that single wreck amounted to a colossal 34,000 birds and over 90 per cent of them were auks. Nearly 5 per cent of the casualties were puffins; in excess of 1,500 were discovered dead and dying. The actual losses would be impossible to estimate. Many birds would have been lost at sea, having sunk to the bottom, and a proportion of others could have been lost to predators. A few birds were found well inland, e.g. one puffin, which had been ringed at the breeding colony in the Orkneys, was retrieved in Bedfordshire.

It is not possible to be certain why these large wrecks of sea birds occur but it appears to be a natural form of mortality. Only comparatively few of the birds are oiled and this may occur after death, as they are being washed ashore. It cannot therefore be associated with the typical oiling problem. Birds that are examined do not appear to be suffering from any disease or chemical pollution. All of the birds found dead in this way are emaciated and in a very poor condition. It is generally considered that the actual death was due to starvation. The dead or dying birds are seriously underweight and birds of all ages are affected equally.

Deaths occur probably as the result of an accumulation of problems associated with stormy weather. During a period of prolonged storms and constant gale-force winds, the puffin may well suffer from the constant battering of the sea and wind. In this tired state, it could then be blown away from the area of its food supply. Finding food hard to capture in the constantly heaving seas, it would find itself even weaker. It is also possible that the turbulent upper layer of water may force the fish deeper and so out of the puffin's reach. Chilled, tired and weak from hunger, the bird is driven by the tide and wind to be washed up, dead, along the tide line.

This apparently natural, but none-the-less sad, form of mortality fortunately does not appear to affect breeding numbers greatly. On the Isle of May, after the 1983 wreck, the percentage mortality was considered to be higher than usual, nevertheless the occupied nesting burrows increased and the colony continued to expand.

The puffin is not only exploited by predators as a direct food source but is also pursued for the fish it carries back to its chick. This behaviour is commonly carried out by the skuas and gulls and it is known as *kleptoparasitism*. This activity is much more than a thieving gull grabbing the odd load of fish from a passing puffin. It is a definite food source and the skuas, particularly the Arctic skua, and some gulls rely on it. They have developed cunning strategies for capturing the tempting fish which the puffin carries. The method adopted by the skuas, which are specialist kleptoparasites, is to try first to intercept the puffin while it is flying in from the ocean. The further away from land the puffin is when first attacked, the more likely the skua is to capture the fish. There are two reasons for this: firstly, the skua has longer to pursue the puffin before it reaches the safety of the colony and its burrow and, secondly, the puffin is much less inclined to shed its load the nearer it is to the colony. The skua pursues a selected puffin, outmanoeuvring it in flight; if still well out to sea, the puffin may drop the load of fish out of fright. The skua instantly breaks off the chase and tries to catch the fish before they hit the sea. It will then land on the water to gather up any remaining fish. If the puffin will not release the fish, the skua may grab at the puffin with its beak and even attempt to snatch the fish. On occasions, Arctic skuas may even cooperate with each other in the pursuit of a puffin. Skuas are not by any means always successful and only about 20 per cent of chased puffins actually drop their fish.

The technique used by the gulls is even less successful, and much more clumsy. The two species of gulls involved are the herring gull and the lesser blackbacked gull. They actually hunt amongst the colony because they have little chance of outmanoeuvring a puffin in flight. They use several techniques and, in every case, have to get within a few metres of the puffin before it is worth their while attempting to intercept the bird. One method is to drift along the cliff top and try to anticipate where an approaching bird is about to land. If the gull guessed correctly then it may be able to grab at the puffin the moment it lands. However, puffins are aware of this and will land right in their burrow entrance and disappear instantly. Other puffins, with less favourable nest sites, are unable to do this and these birds are more vulnerable. It may be necessary for the puffin to abort its attempt to land and to turn back over the sea. It is possible that the gull if it is close enough, will give chase but if the puffin is able to use gravity to gain speed, the gull has little chance of capturing it. Other gulls will wait in ambush near an anticipated landing area. As the puffin arrives to land, it will leap to intercept it. Sometimes the gull may get a grasp of the puffin's tail or wing and feathers will fly as the puffin struggles to escape. The puffin is loath to drop its load of fish and will attempt to enter its burrow with the gull trying to drag it out. Quite often a few fish are dropped in the struggles and the gull will break off to eat them before another gull shares the plunder. In some locations, the gulls appear to work specific territories, which they defend, whilst in others they are more at random.

As the puffins fly into the bay, gulls may be waiting in ambush on prominent rocks. The puffin flies the gauntlet of hungry thieves and may fly temptingly close to one of the gulls. The gull might pursue it and, very occasionally, if the puffin is caught by surprise, may even force the bird to drop the fish. In general, the puffin only releases the fish at the last moment; its first reaction is to lose height rapidly and thus gain speed. Only if the gull is close behind when the puffin is a metre or two above the water will it drop its load; it cannot dive beneath the water when flying at full speed. It is not uncommon to see a gull standing in the middle of the colony with several puffins waiting for it to move, so that they can walk over to their burrows and deliver their load. The watching gull knows that they are too far away to attack successfully and the puffins dare not move any closer for fear of the consequences. The deadlock is broken when one puffin moves temptingly closer and the gull begins to respond. Instantly, all the puffins scramble over the cliff and the gull is left to drift on to another part of the colony.

When watching a colony, the effects of kleptoparasitism seems to be a severe problem to the puffins in some areas. One can get the impression that the chicks underground will receive a severely reduced ration as a result of these activities. Research has shown that, in a heavily parasitised colony, up to 19 per cent of puffins may lose their fish to the gulls. However, the success of fledging, in general, is unimpaired. The most likely puffins to suffer are those which have difficult access to their burrows. As a result, the colonies that nest on flat ground are usually more affected by the gulls' piratical activities.

In the course of this chapter, we have seen the natural problems that the puffins face, at sea and at the colony. The balance between pirate, predator and puffin is stable; it is nature's method of population control, of both predator and prey. There is one predator that we have not yet discussed and that is Man.

7 Men and Puffins

IT seems inevitable that Man plays a significant role in the life or death of the puffin. Human beings have preyed upon puffins as a source of food since records were kept. In this, Man could be regarded as a natural predator. However, human beings also have an affection for the puffin, giving it a variety of local names and spinning yarns about its life style. Men valued the bird as a source of food and knew exactly what the puffin was worth in terms of cash.

Today we do not have such values to apply but it would seem worthwhile to decide on the value of a sea-bird colony in conservation terms. Only a few sea-bird colonies are now preyed on by Man but human activities will probably determine the balance between success and disaster for puffins. The most obvious threat at Man's disposal is oil.

Man's affection for the puffin is illustrated in some of the local names. I have heard it referred to as 'Tom Noddy', a name which originated in the Farne Islands, and 'Tammie Norie' and 'Coulter Neb' were also in regular use in local communities. The word 'neb' refer to its beak, whilst 'coulter' refers to the shape of the beak. Its beak gave the puffin a variety of names, including 'Bottlenose', 'Sea Parrot' or simply 'Bill'. Some people clearly thought the puffin belonged only to their area and named it accordingly; 'Bass Cock' or 'Ailsa Parrot' are two examples and, in Yorkshire, it was referred to as the 'Flamborough Head Pilot'. The name 'Lundi' or 'Lunda' occurs as a Faeroese name and originated in Iceland and Norway. Thus Lundy Island in the Bristol Channel is so-called because of the presence of the puffin and the affection in which it was held. The name 'Puffin' derives from the word 'puffing' and is related mainly to the chick and to the local habit of eating the chicks of both puffins and Manx shearwaters. 'Puff' suggests something that is fat or swollen and this certainly applies to these chicks. People collecting the chicks for food did not bother to distinguish between the two species; they both nest beneath the ground in burrows and look and taste much the same. Puffin is the accepted common name for the bird. The Manx shearwater retains part of its history in the scientific name of *Puffinus puffinus*.

Wherever large colonies of puffins existed, Man has exploited the bird as an abundant source of food. It would seem that, as early as 1337, the Scilly Isles were rented for 6 shillings and 8 pence (67p in today's currency). The alternative to this payment was to supply 300 puffins; the value of three puffins was therefore about one old penny. Bearing in mind that at least two puffins would be needed to provide a meal for one person and the value of a penny at that time, puffins were highly esteemed by some landowners. Other members of the aristocracy considered them only suitable for servants. Coastal villages and island communities relied heavily on the annual crop of sea birds, including puffins. Men were not slow to use their inventive minds and their knowledge of the puffin's habits to devise a variety of methods of capturing their prey. One rather clumsy and time-consuming method was used early in the season, soon after the puffins had laid their eggs. Occupied burrows were located, either by watching the arrival of the birds or by using a dog. The fowler then attempted to hook the puffin out of the burrow with a metal hook attached to a rod. Because the tunnels would bend in any direction, and many burrows would be too long, the fowler would dig down to the burrow and try his luck with the hook again. This crude method of capture meant that many burrows were damaged but the fowlers were eager to protect their annual supply of food and, as a result, only cropped an area every 3 years. The eggs would also be removed if they could be reached. Men would use this method of capture early in the season, when stocks of meat were low or when they required a little variety of diet after a winter of dried or salted meat. Generally only a few birds were harvested in this way but eight Faeroe Islanders are known to have collected in excess of 1,300 birds in a single day in 1942.

It is during the second half of June and July that the puffin numbers in the colony are at their peak. Therefore it was at this time that the fowlers concentrated their efforts on the puffins. A pole was used, 3 to 4 metres long. The end of the pole was forked and between the fork was slung a netting bag. This piece of equipment was known as a *fleygastong* or *fleyg* and it was the skilful use of this that enabled a great many puffins to be captured. Knowing the habits of the puffins, the fowler would select a windy day and a location where large numbers of birds gathered. If he were to decoy the area with a few dead birds, the puffins would consider the landing area to be safe. The net was laid flat on the ground while the fowler held the other end of the pole. As the birds approached upwind and slowed over the landing spot, the fowler was able expertly and quickly to lift the fleyg and scoop the puffin out of the air. The bird's neck was pulled and it was placed on the growing pile of puffins behind the man. He was ready in moments for the next puffin. In skilful hands, the fleyg could remove hundreds of puffins in a day and one man could average 250–300 birds. On extremely good days, an expert may even capture and kill in the region of 1,000 birds, the record claimed is 1,201. The peak of activity was about 50–100 years ago, when Faeroe Islanders harvested approximately 300,000 puffins per annum and a similar number was also gathered in Iceland. Despite these huge numbers, the success of the puffin was not diminished, which gives an indication of the size of the colonies. In general, fowlers took pride in avoiding birds that were carrying fish so that they could continue to feed their young. It would be fair to assume that the majority of birds caught were sub-adults. They would be abundant in July and constantly flying around the colony, whereas the adults would be flying in with fish and aiming directly down their burrows.

The technique favoured by the inhabitants of St Kilda relied on the puffin's curiosity. A long flexible pole was used with a noose attached to the end. The noose was gently slid along the ground towards the unfortunate victim but, instead of retreating, the puffin's curiosity compelled it to take a closer look at this strange but apparently harmless object. With a deft twist of the wrist the man would flip the noose over the puffin's head before quickly removing the bird, so that its alarm did not disturb the rest of the group. Once again hundreds of birds could be captured in this way in a single day. A variety of other methods that involved nooses were also used, including covering a floating raft of wood with nooses made of horse hair. A puffin which landed on the raft would become ensnared and its struggles would attract other inquisitive birds. They, in turn, also fell victim to the nooses. Long rows of nooses were arranged along the colony slopes and trapped birds by their legs as they pottered amongst the burrows.

Nets were also used in a variety of ways and usually trapped a high percentage of breeding birds. One method used was to cover the burrows at night in order to capture the adults as they left the nest in the morning after incubating the egg or young chick. Another method involved two men, who carried a net suspended between poles; they would move up the slopes, holding the net close to the ground, towards the resting puffins. As the puffins took fright and fled to the sea, the men would raise the poles, capturing many birds in the net. In other areas, people simply knocked puffins out of the air using poles. On occasions, dogs have been trained to gather puffins; these were used at night to retrieve the young, fat chicks as they left their burrows for the sea. Puffins were also shot for 'sport' but, with so many birds wheeling about, one wonders from where the skill or pleasure was derived. Fishermen once shot puffins to bait lobster pots and one local man informed me that a single shot from a 12-bore gun could supply up to twenty puffins for the next day's pots.

The flesh of a puffin is dark and only the breast provides any appreciable amount of meat. As a result, a man could easily eat two or even three puffins in a meal. The bird may have been braised, boiled or stuffed and roasted; once cooked the flesh had no taste of fish. In some areas it was permissible to eat puffin meat on Fridays; presumably because it lived exclusively on fish it was regarded as a fish/bird. I would imagine that puffins were not exploited for their flesh by the Irish, for it is claimed that the puffins contain the reincarnated spirits of the monks that lived on the islands. Many birds would have been preserved for the months when fresh protein was not available and these were often salted in brine. Alternatively, they may have been plucked, smoked in barrels of burning peat and hung to dry in the beams of the fowler's cottages. In areas where puffins were sold, most of the meat was pickled in vinegar before being transported. Puffin eggs were collected and eaten, but not to the same extent as those of many other seabirds. The reason for this was due to the difficulty in collecting them, rather than their palatability. The taste for the eggs had to be acquired; some people regarded them as a delicacy, whilst others considered them to be most unpalatable.

I have written this chapter as if the annual puffin harvests were history. Indeed, in the British Isles, the Protection of Birds Act prevented the legal killing of puffins and the Wildlife and Countryside Act 1981 continues the protection. All countries that have breeding colonies have protected this bird for many years and, in most situations, they are totally protected throughout the breeding season. In Iceland and the Faeroe Islands, the birds are still hunted but strict legislation ensures that the population of puffins is not overexploited.

However, it would be foolish to be over-sentimental about the killing of puffins, provided it is controlled and forms an important supply of food for local communities. The life of many of these communities revolves around the sea-bird harvest and the conservation of the villager's life style can go hand in hand with the conservation of puffins. Years of research have failed to show that the puffin population has been adversely affected by the traditional hunting of sea birds. It is not traditional Man that threatens the environment; it is modern Man.

Ten years ago it was stated that well in excess of 1,800 million tonnes of oil were transported across the sea each year and it was claimed that 1.6 million tonnes was wasted or lost into the ocean. Since that time, the demand for oil has doubled that figure and over 60 per cent of the tonnage transported by sea is now oil. Regularly we hear of major oil spills into the ocean as the result of an oil-well calamity or tanker wreck. There are also, almost daily, spillages of a more minor nature, where pipes are broken, accidents occur or tanks are cleaned out and washed into the sea. All major oil spills are accidents; no one would deny that fact, but it is frightening to consider the potential danger we are moving across the ocean, at the whim of the weather and human fallibility. The attitude towards the so-called 'minor' incidents are of equal concern, where oil is deliberately washed into the sea to empty a tank, for example, and when tanks are cleaned out or sea-water ballast from tanks previously used for oil is disposed of. In some ways, I am more concerned about the attitude than the oil. In general, I tend to believe that once Man is aware of the problem he will work towards solving the situation. I hope I shall not be disappointed on this occasion.

The facts related to puffins are not as bad as one at first imagines, although the evidence is difficult to gather. More major oil spills occur during the winter, presumably as a result of winter storms, so it is to the puffin's advantage that it winters spread out across the North Atlantic. The main dangers occur when numbers of birds are congregated together in specific areas. It would seem that far fewer puffins are oiled than any other auks; some figures indicate that only 1.5 per cent of auks found affected were puffins. This may be because puffins are more widely dispersed but it is more likely that, when oiled, they are further away from land and are therefore less likely to be washed ashore and found by ornithologists. In an experiment, 410 dead, oiled auks were dumped into the Irish Sea; each bird was marked and searches were made along the coast to find them. Only 82 of the sample were found (i.e. 20 per cent); the rest were thought to have sunk and, in fact, one was recovered from the sea floor. In 1967, the oil tanker *Torrey Canyon* spilled an enormous tonnage of oil into the sea off the Cornish coast but, out of the thousands of auks found dead on the beaches, only a very few puffins were recovered. The effect, however, was to reduce the population of puffin breeding on the French coast to only 16 per cent of the previous figure. One island had a population of 2,500 pairs; it was left with 400 pairs and that was halved when the next oil spillage occurred in that area. The French colonies were declining already when the oil sealed their fate. It is only these colonies that can claim a genuine, long-term destruction as a result of oil. It is the magnitude of the threat that is of concern; so far puffins have been very lucky.

While writing this book, I heard over the coastguard radio that an oil tanker had grounded about 30 kilometres to the west of Skomer Island. It was July and the middle of the breeding season and, as I looked out of my window, the puffins were flying in from the sea and covering the slopes around me. The wind was from the west and the horror of an oil spill, so close and at this time of year, struck me hard. The next morning seemed the same as usual but, at about 2 p.m., the first slightly oiled bird arrived. It stood on the cliff top with a dark black area on its chest and flank and its beak was smeared with oil from

An oiled puffin is
washed up on the
beach.

trying to preen itself clean. I felt very angry and incredibly useless. More birds arrived during the afternoon with varying amounts of oil and I constantly received conflicting reports about the amount of oil spilt and its direction of travel. It was not long before the oil slick was visible from my window only about a kilometre out from the bay where several thousand birds were nesting and sub-adults were in courtship. As dead and dying puffins struggled into the bay completely blacked with oil I could have screamed with frustration. It seemed inevitable that the oil would fill the bay; already the odd globule was near the landing steps. Beneath me the bay was loaded with puffins, I could only imagine the worst. The weather changed overnight, I hardly dared look out of the window. Apparently the choppy water broke up the slick and the oil dispersed out of harm's way. The puffins escaped with only a few hundred dead, no more than 5 per cent of the population, and the breeding season continued. It had been an accident and everyone had tried very hard to correct the mistake but they could do nothing. At the time I was emotionally involved, today I look back on it and realise just how lucky we were. An incident like that could, next time, wipe out the puffins of Skomer and Skokholm entirely. Surely, if men are clever enough to drill holes in the sea bed to remove oil, we should have the ability to deal with oil spills. Improving methods of dealing with oil spills would be money well spent. Years ago puffins were worth three for a penny. Looking out of my window now, I wonder what they are worth today?

Appendices

Photographic Techniques

PUFFINS are delightful little characters to photograph. Not only are they visually appealing but they are also very easy subjects. There can be few photographers interested in birds who have left a puffin-inhabited island without a handful of attractive photographs. It would seem, therefore, a fairly simple task to take a series of pictures to illustrate this book. However, the aim was to show the many different aspects of the bird's behaviour and to produce a few unusual pictures.

The equipment used for most of the photographs was fairly simple. The camera bodies were 35mm single lens reflex and a range of lenses, from 28mm wide-angle to 300mm telephoto, were used. All the lenses were of fixed focal length and 90 per cent of the photographs were taken with the camera on a tripod.

Portraits of puffins are very simple to take. Late in the season, the birds become very confiding and a little patience, whilst waiting at a favourite landing area, will be rewarded with birds only a couple of metres away. There may be dozens of birds about, so it is often possible to pick and choose the best subjects. The main problem to overcome is contrast: the colouring of the puffin is a mixture of glossy black and pure white and there is detail in both to be captured. As a result, careful exposure setting is most important. For this type of situation, Kodachrome 64 was used but, in situations where capturing action was more important than capturing detail, Ektachrome 200 was preferred. In a location where the birds had become accustomed to my presence, I had one puffin within 20 centimetres of my foot. Many portraits were taken with a 300mm lens but it was quite possible to fill the frame using a 100mm lens.

The problem with using a long-focal-length lens to photograph birds is that the background is left out of focus. In effect, the bird is separated from its environment. To overcome this, and to create a more imaginative picture, some of the photographs were taken with a 28mm wide-angle lens. I found it was possible to edge towards the puffins whilst lying on my stomach. When I was within a metre of the birds, it was worth taking a picture and then I would edge even closer until I was only a few centimetres away. The same principles could be used when photographing groups of birds, both with telephoto and wide-angle lenses. The inquisitive nature of the puffin can be employed to attract a bird towards you. On one occasion, a puffin was curious about a camera that I had left on the ground a few metres away. It pottered over to inspect it and even pecked at the strap. I have even been known to sit on the rocks, singing to the puffins on the water; I can only assume it was the birds inquisitiveness that made them paddle towards me, rather than their appreciation of music!

Close-up photographs on the water are not easy to achieve. The puffin is never still, paddling this way and that, bobbing up and down on the smallest of waves. Not only does a telephoto lens magnify the image, it also magnifies the movement within the picture. In most water pictures, a fast shutter speed was selected to overcome this problem.

We have seen that a proportion of the puffin's courtship, as well as copulation, takes place on the sea. To capture this seemed an extremely difficult task. Finding a pair of birds mating somewhere on the ocean, within range of a lens, on a sunny day and facing in the right direction, appeared almost impossible. I was able to borrow a huge 1200mm lens from Nikon UK Ltd but even so the puffin still had to be very close. It was incredibly difficult to keep the lens from vibrating in the gusting winds, even on my very heavy tripod. For 3 days I crouched on the rocks on the edge of the bay, photographing the puffins in courtship and copulation. In those few days, I watched pair after pair through the camera lens. When watching puffins, it is so easy to be distracted by the number of birds present. One's eyes cannot help straying to other active birds. Concentrating through the camera lens, it was possible to follow a pair for over half an hour and to carefully observe the build-up to copulation.

The photographs I most enjoyed attempting involved getting into the water with the puffins. I invented a housing into which I could safely put my camera for photographing under water. The housing needed to be large because I required it to house the camera body, motor drive and a 100mm lens (there was also room for a small flash unit). The camera could be electrically-triggered through the housing by a watertight button and I could focus via a rubber sleeve made from the thumb of a rubber glove. The unit was just buoyant and I needed plenty of weight around my waist to enable me to get beneath the water in my wetsuit. As I swam across the bay towards the puffins, I felt that I must be swimming exceptionally fast until I realised that they were swimming towards me! Puffins began to land all around me from other parts of the bay and I was surrounded by birds about 2 metres away. The pleasure I received from the experience far out-

weighed the few photographs that were usable. It was only possible to take photographs in the clearest water and most of the time it looked like soup through the lens. I took the opportunity of photographing the birds from the water surface, giving a puffin-eye view of a puffin!

Photographing birds in flight must be a film manufacturer's dream. Rolls and rolls of film must be wasted in sea-bird colonies each year but it seems to be the only way of getting a few reasonable pictures. Two things can help: firstly, a steady wind for the birds to float on and, secondly, a good knowledge of the subject. I anticipated the flight path of the bird, or a particular landing spot, then with the pan head loose on the tripod, followed the bird until it was in focus.

Puffins are one of the few birds that can be successfully photographed without using a hide. However, for certain behaviour pictures, a hide was used so that the birds behaved perfectly naturally. To achieve low-angle photographs, the hide was dug into the ground so that the camera lens was a few centimetres above ground level.

Studying and photographing the puffins underground was one of the most frustrating yet rewarding times that I have spent. Having carefully removed the side of the nest burrow and covered the excavation with lightproof material, I then lay flat on my stomach peering into the darkness. The canvas covering reached from the opened burrow over my head and right down to my feet. It was totally black in

121

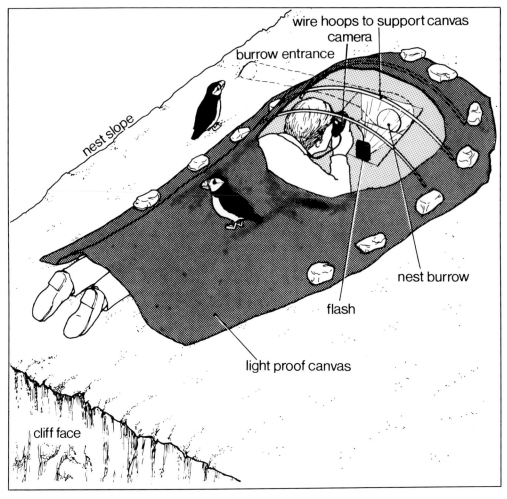

wire hoops to support canvas
camera
burrow entrance
nest slope
nest burrow
flash
light proof canvas
cliff face

the burrow and it was necessary to use a torch to pre-focus the camera. The camera was held on a mini tripod rammed into the ground and a flash was situated nearby. After about 5 minutes it was possible to make out the shape of the chick and after a further 5 or 10 minutes it was amazing how clearly I could see. The chick would entertain me for several minutes and then would rest and I would have to wait for hours on end in the gloom. My eyes were fixed on the light filtering down the burrow, in the hope that it would darken, as the body of the adult filled the tunnel. One day I spent about 13 hours underground and I didn't take one picture. At that time I did not think the bird was relaxed with the arrangement I had made and so I felt it was wise simply to enjoy the observation and not to press the shutter. My interest has always been with wildlife and I use the camera to record the things that I observe. There can be no excuse for disturbing

Photographing the puffin in the nest burrow.

122

wildlife subjects for the sake of a photograph. The adult birds accepted the modified burrow and behaved naturally, rearing the chick in good time. My previous experience with nest photography underground somehow exaggerated the frustrations in the puffin burrow. I had used a similar technique when taking photographs for my book on the kingfisher. These birds visited the nest chamber about 100 times a day; the puffin only visited the youngster on a handful of occasions. Having waited for about 3 hours, I began to wonder if I could be disturbing the adults but was reassured when a puffin landed on my head (which was beneath the canvas). It proceeded to walk down my back and sat on my bottom for 10 minutes. I could hear puffins all around me and on several occasions they landed on me, especially in the evenings. I must make it quite clear that it is illegal to disturb the nest of any wild bird in many countries. In Britain, to undertake a project such as this it is necessary to obtain permission from the Nature Conservancy Council.

For the birdwatcher and photographer alike, the puffin is an exciting little character. The environment of the cliff tops, the atmosphere of a sea-bird colony and guaranteed close views of puffins ensure that a trip to a large puffin colony is an exciting day. If one is interested in photography or watching birds, there can be few birds that are more obliging than the comical puffin.

Distribution of the Atlantic Puffin

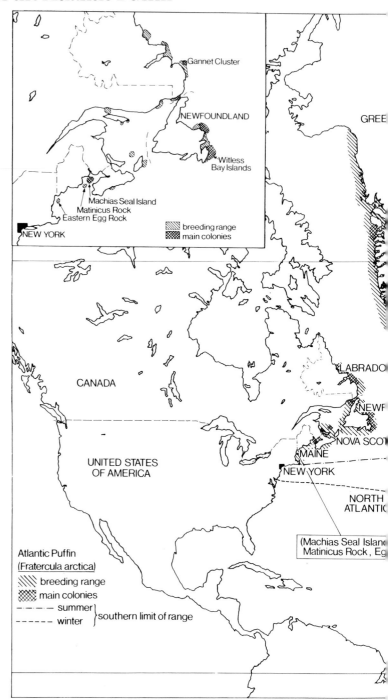

Map showing the breeding range, main colonies and southern limits of the summer and winter ranges of the Atlantic puffin (*Fratercula arctica*).

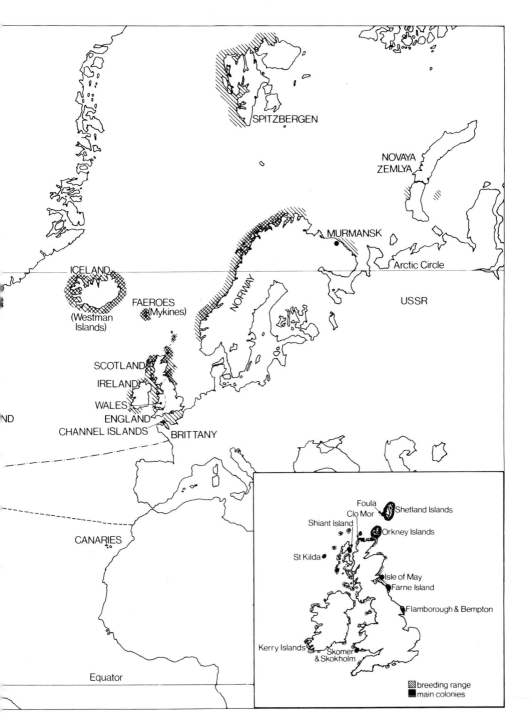

SPITZBERGEN

NOVAYA
ZEMLYA

MURMANSK

Arctic Circle

ICELAND

(Westman
Islands)

FAEROES
(Mykines)

NORWAY

USSR

SCOTLAND

IRELAND

WALES

ND

ENGLAND

CHANNEL ISLANDS

BRITTANY

CANARIES

Foula
Clo Mor   Shetland Islands
Shiant Island
                Orkney Islands
St Kilda

                Isle of May
                Farne Island

                Flamborough & Bempton

Equator

Kerry Islands
        Skomer
        & Skokholm

⬚⬚ breeding range
■ main colonies

Further Reading

ASHCROFT, R.E. (1976) *Breeding Biology and Survival of Puffins* D.Phil. thesis, Oxford. (Unpublished)

BUREAU, L. (1877) 'De la mue du bec et des ornaments palpebraux' *Bull. Soc. Zool. Fr.* **2**: 377–399.

CORKHILL, P. (1972) 'Measurements of puffins as criteria of sex and age' *Bird Study* **19**: 193–201.

CORKHILL, P. (1973) 'Food and feeding ecology of puffins' *Bird Study* **20**: 207–220.

GREENOAK, F. (1979) *All the Birds of the Air* André Deutsch Ltd, London.

HARRIS, M.P. (1976) 'The present status of the puffin in Britain and Ireland' *British Birds* **69**: 239–264.

HARRIS, M. (1979) 'Measurements and weights of British puffins' *Bird Study* **26**: 179–186.

HARRIS, M.P. (1984) *The Puffin* T. and A.D. Poyser, Calton, Staffordshire.

HUDSON, P.J. (1979) 'The parent–chick feeding relationship of the puffin' *J. Anim. Ecol.* **48**: 889–898.

KIESS, S.W. (1978–82) *Egg Rock Up-date* National Audubon Society, Ithaca.

LOCKLEY, R.M. (1953) *Puffins* Dent, London.

Index

Page numbers in *italics* refer to illustrations.

ageing *22, 23, 25*
aggression 49, *57, 58, 58*, 59
Ashcroft, Ruth 66
auks 18, 115

Bay of Biscay 42
beak 21, *21, 22, 23, 25*, 36–37, 56, 57, *58, 62*, 69, *70, 74, 75*, 83
billing 11, 17, 49, 69, *71, 72*–81
bracken 44, 46
British Isles 27–29, 41–66, 78–82, 114, 123, *125*
burrows 15, 16, *41*, 44, 45, 48, 59, 67, 69, 78, *80*, 81–83, *83*, 84–90, *92*, 94
  location 44–46
  loyalty 16, 66–67, 69
  photography 121–122, *122*, *122*–123

call 64–65, 87
  chick 90
camera 51, 119–120, *121*, 122
camouflage 34
Canada 24, 27, 42, *124*
Channel Islands 27, *125*
chick 78, 82–84, *84*, 85, *85*, 86, *86*, 87–99, 101, 110
  feeding 84–87, 90–92, *92*, 93, 94
  growth rate 84, 87, 94, 95
Clo Mor 29, *125*
colony *10, 14, 15, 16, 26, 43*, 44, 45, *45*, 46, *46*, 47, *47*, 48–65, *80*
copulation 72, 73–74, *74*, 75–77, 120
Corkhill, Peter 67
courtship 11, 69–71, *71*, 72, *73, 73, 74, 75*, 75–77, 80, 81, 120

description 19–20, *20*, 21
diet 34

digging 44, 47, 69–70, *70*, 71–72, 95
displacement activity 39, 76
distribution
  breeding 24–29, *124*
  winter 30, 39–42, *124*
dominant display 17, *54–55, 56, 56–57*, 64
Dorset 28
dummy puffins 27

egg 77, 78, 80, 82, 94, 191, 114
  hatching 82
  laying 68
  replacement 80, 97
  size 78
Egg Rock *124*
  Eastern 27–47, *124*
  Western 27
environment 30, *32–33*, 42–43, 78–100
excrement 93
eye adornments 19, 23, 24

Faeroes 27, 66, 112–113, 114, *125*
Fair Isle 29
Farn Islands 28, 47, 48, 72, *125*
feeding 12, 37, 63
feet 15, 19, *20*, 23, 30, 31, 34, 36, 57, 59, *61*, 64–72, 83
fighting 57–58, *58*, 59
film 119, 121
fish 12, 34, 36, 37, *60, 62*, 88–89, *91, 92*, 109
fledglings 31, 95–96, *96*, 97, *97*, 98, *98*, 99, 101, 110
fleyg 112
flight 15, 31, 39, 51, 63, 121
  taking off 44, 63, *63*
Foula 29, *125*
fowling 112–114
France 27, 115, *125*

gaping *54–55*, 56, 57, 58, 59

Grassholm 48
Greenland 24, 27, 66, 78, 82, *124*,
gulls 9, 51, 64, 87, 97–100, 103–104,
    104, 105, 106, 109–110

habitat *10*
Harris, Dr Mike 24, 100
head flicking 11, 57, 73, *73*, 77
head jerking 56, 57
hide 121
horned puffin 19

Iceland 24, 41, 66, 114, *125*
incubation 68, *79*, 79–80, 82
Ireland 28, *125*
Isle of May 28, 29, 47–108, *125*

jackdaws 106

kleptoparasitism 51, 108–110

Labrador 27, *124*
landing
    on land *14, 48, 50*, 51, 52, *52, 60*
    on water 31
lens 120
life span 100–101
local names 111

Machias Seal Island 27, *124*
Maine 27, *124*
mammals 102
Manx shearwaters 107
mate loyalty 66–67, 76, 80
Matinicus Rock 27, *124*
Mediterranean Sea 24, 42
mortality 40, 52
moulting 39, 96
Mykines 27, *125*

nest material 64, *77*, 77–78, 84, *85*, 86
Newfoundland 27–78, *124*
North Atlantic 9, 24, 30, 34, 41–66,
    115, *124–125*
Norway 24, 27, 41, 78, *125*

oil 39, 100, 114–115, *116*, 117
Orkneys 29, *125*

pair formation 49, 72, 81
penguin 18
photography 51, 119–122, *122*, 123
pollution 100
population 24–29, 30
    dynamics 100
predators 31, 44, 51, 82, 87, 90,

95–97, 100, 101–103, *103*, 104, *104*,
    105
preen gland 38, *61*
preening 9, *38*, 38–39, *60*, *61*, 62–69,
    75

rabbits 44
rafts 11, *13*, 66
rhinoceros auklet 19
ringing 40–41, *41*, 47, 101
roosting *40*, 62
Røst 27

St Kilda 29, 113, *125*
salt extraction 37–38
Scilly Isles 112
Scotland 28, 29, 47, 66, *125*
sexing 23, 24
Shetland 29, *125*
Shiant 29, *125*
shooting 27, 40
size 19, 24
Skokholm 28, *125*
Skomer Island *10*, 18, 28, 66, 115, *125*
skuas 109
Spitzbergen 24, 27, *125*
sub-adults *25*, 46, 49, 51, 57, 62, 64,
    81, 90
sub-colony 44, 68
submissiveness 53, *53*
subspecies 24
swimming 30

taking off
    land *63*
    water *13*
Torrey Canyon 115
tufted puffin 19

underwater 12, 34, *35*, 36–37, 39,
    120, *121*
upright walk 56, *56*
USA 24, 27, 47, *124*
USSR 27, *125*

Wales 28, *125*
weight 24
    chick 83, 93–94, 95–96
Westman Islands 24, *124–125*
wheeling *50*, 51, 62
wings 24, 31, *35*, 36, 39, 58, *61*, 63,
    75, 85, *98*
    flapping *75*, 76
winter 9, 23–24, 30, 39–43, 67, 101,
    115
wrecks 107–108

THE
PUFFIN

With its brightly striped bill and pristine black-and-white plumage, the Common or Atlantic Puffin (*Fratercula arctica*) is one of the most popular and most easily identified seabirds of the northern hemisphere. This comical little bird is found in colonies on the rocky sea cliffs and offshore islands of the northern USA, Canada, Greenland, Iceland, the USSR, Norway, Northern Europe and the United Kingdom. This book provides a detailed study of the natural history of the puffin and gives valuable insight into its feeding, breeding and travelling habits, courtship and social behaviour. There is information on breeding colonies and on the dangers puffins face from predators, including human activity and that twentieth-century killer – oil pollution.

The book is illustrated with over 70 colour photographs, specially taken by the authors, which show previously unseen and fascinating shots, both underwater and underground.

Cover photographs by David Boag
and Mike Alexander

£12.99

Printed in Hong Kong

ISBN 0-7137-2596-6

9 780713 725964 >